HOW TO BREAK UNHEALTHY EMOTIONAL PATTERNS

The **RADIAR** Process

for Stopping Self-Sabotage, Gaining Confidence After Years of Being Silent, and Getting Free from Overthinking

Andrea Alvarado

Heureka Resources

How To Break Unhealthy Emotional Patterns *The RADIAR Process for Stopping Self-Sabotage, Gaining Confidence After Years of Being Silent, and Getting Free from Overthinking*

Author: Andrea Alvarado

First English edition — 2026. Originally published in Spanish — 2025. Published by Heureka Resources LLC Florida, United States

ISBN: 979-8-9937842-4-3

Library of Congress Control Number: 2026912897

Translated from the Spanish original by Heureka Resources LLC

Foreword: Teresa Baró

Design and layout: Heureka Resources LLC

Printed in the United States of America.

For Emma.

Table of Contents

Foreword

Reading this book may lead you to a life of true luxury.

You might assume this is just another marketing slogan, the kind a guru uses to sell a course or a book. But it's quite the opposite.

Today, luxury means being able to focus on what truly matters: having clarity of direction, shaping yourself as your own potter, learning from experience, and adapting to changing circumstances.

And the key is to do it without imitating anyone else, from a place of authenticity, and without handing over responsibility to a guide who charts the path for us. There is no need for gurus.

RADIAR invites you to become your own guide. You will ask the questions, challenge the answers, make decisions, get things right or wrong, and examine yourself honestly, always ready to start again. As the author suggests, life is a continuous and deliberate act of choosing. There are no guaranteed happy endings, but each day offers a new opportunity to choose the life you want.

In a world of distraction and superficiality, of stress and appearances, isn't it a rare privilege to truly know yourself and live with autonomy and coherence?

Isn't it a worthy aim to leave this world with the peace of mind that comes from having lived authentically and given your best?

In moments of unease, failure, or confusion, we all look for an anchor for our hopes. It is easy to believe in magical solutions, especially when they are presented through stories of dazzling success. Many claim to have overcome a life crisis—or at least appear to have—and go on to share their formula for success with the world. That becomes their livelihood.

But what part of yourself have you set aside in trying to fit into someone else's model?

Only you can discover your reasons, define your goals, and make your decisions. RADIAR offers you the tools. Read it, reread it, underline it, keep a notebook close—and write.

Teresa Baró

Writer and communication specialist

Introduction

If you are reading these lines, you have probably already tried other paths: you have tried different methods, paid for courses, and followed someone else's instructions. And yet, here you are. Still searching.

Now is the time to ask yourself: How much have you spent trying to find outside yourself what can only be found within?

I want to be clear from the outset: this is not a self-help manual. It does not aim to complete or change you, nor will it sell you absolute certainties or magic steps. Rather, it is a firm and necessary reminder that you already have everything you need.

Have you ever questioned whether the existence you defend is truly yours, or whether it reflects what others expect of you?

Although the question seems simple, the answer is not. Time is a finite account—one that cannot be replenished; no one knows for sure how much they have left, but we all consume a portion of it every day.

The critical point is that many people waste this irreplaceable resource fulfilling expectations instead of pursuing their own desires.

This book is based on experience: on successes and mistakes, on lessons learned from people of integrity and others who were not so honorable; it draws from psychology and introspection. But you don't need my story as proof; all you need is the willingness to face your own.

Here you will find questions, not recipes, reflections rather than solutions. Because the experience that matters is yours. Only you know what you must do—or not do.

RADIAR was born from this premise. This process is presented as a diagram you can return to whenever you lose perspective. It does not seek to transform you, but rather to give you back your own image, undistorted. Transformation, if it occurs, will be your work.

To organize what you are about to read, I propose a six-stage framework that you will find at the center of the book, accompanied by "The Record," a space designed to anchor your reflections in your life.

I should warn you: this is not a text to read in one sitting or to collect as a series of underlined phrases. It is a space where you will pause to think. Genuine questions—the ones that chart your course—can only be asked by you.

I wrote this so that you can look at yourself without filters. So that you can choose yourself again and again and fully inhabit your own space—not that of others.

If you expect someone else to fix your life for you, close these pages now. If you are willing to observe yourself without embellishment and move forward without guarantees, keep going.

There is no "later"; the opportunity you have is this one—the one you choose now.

This book does not seek to "empower" you. No one can give you power, because there is nothing essential that you lack. Power is not granted; it is reclaimed.

The very notion of empowerment stems from a misguided perspective: those who seek to empower others place themselves a step above them, assuming greater clarity and offering an authority that never belonged to them. This act, even when well-intentioned, conceals a subtle form of condescension, as it is based on the false premise that people are incomplete or need to be "fixed."

People are not incomplete. They may be tired, confused, or caught in inertia, but that is not a deficiency or a structural defect; it is, simply, part of being human.

Genuine respect does not lie in giving power, but in not taking it away. Nor does it lie in taking the place of the one who must decide, but in seeing the other as an equal—fully capable of seeing, choosing, and standing on their own.

This work operates under one axiom: authority is an inherent and inalienable condition; it is not something to be sought—it is claimed and exercise

Section 1 - The Starting Point

Information is everywhere.

Wisdom is built within.

CHAPTER 1: The Guru Who Needs You Lost

There is a pattern. Someone goes through personal hell, comes out the other side, and decides that their mission is to save others from that same suffering. The story is compelling, and the intention seems genuine. However, something doesn't quite fit. To make sense, that savior needs you to be broken. They need your helplessness to justify their guidance.

Who have you allowed to occupy that place in your life?

They don't always appear with the label "guru." Sometimes it's a partner, a boss, or a mentor—in short, anyone whose opinion you've placed above your own. Little by little, that person takes over your judgment, until you reach the point of doubting everything except them.

Their identity depends on people following them, paying them, and validating them—without your approval, they don't exist. This creates a perverse dynamic: the more you depend on them, the more their value is affirmed. The more you believe you need their method, the more successful their message appears. It's a cruel balance: your fragility sustains their strength, and your confusion becomes the fuel that justifies their vision.

Who have you followed who has made you feel that, without their guidance, you are doomed to failure?

The problem is not helping from experience but turning that help into a business that requires permanent disciples. There is a fundamental difference: an ethical doctor or therapist works to discharge you and restore your autonomy; the guru works to ensure you never leave. Because if they truly showed you that you can stand on your own and recognized your ability, they would cease to be indispensable. And if they ceased to be indispensable, the entire model would collapse. Instead of reminding you of your inner authority, they need to remind you of your lack. They need you to doubt yourself.

It is in this scenario that the narrative is reversed: what you have done is no longer enough; you must move on to the next level. That course is no longer enough—you now need an annual membership. And so, each achievement comes with a new flaw that you must resolve: you finish one stage only to discover another layer, a deeper trauma, a limiting belief, or something defective that only they can help you see.

The story of overcoming adversity becomes a credential—and bait. It may appear as a testimonial on a sales page, a polished video telling their "before and after," or a stream of perfect images that seem to prove that if you follow in their footsteps, your life will also fall into place.

"I was where you are." That phrase acts as an emotional bridge that instantly builds trust. And from that trust comes dependence: if they were able to get out, they must know the way. And if they know the way, you convince yourself that you need them, so you don't get lost.

But there is a catch: their path is not yours, and their hell is not yours.

The circumstances, resources, and context that shaped their journey are not the same as yours. That experience, however honest it may be, does not become a universal guide—yet it still offers you certainties. It tells you what to do, how to feel, and what your experiences mean. There is no room for your own interpretation, your own pace, or your own way of processing. If they admitted that each person is unique, the method would lose its effectiveness. Universal formulas sell; uniqueness does not.

Then there is the other side of the same coin: the successful role model who sells not past suffering, but projected success. The one who appears "outstanding," "fabulous," and "wealthy." They sell you the formula for achieving their success, but it is often completely incongruous: they claim to teach you how to build a successful business while theirs is barely surviving. They are trapped in the image they project and need you to desire that image to sustain it.

The savior wants to be indispensable. And to do that, they must remind you of everything you have not yet achieved, everything you lack, and the ways in which you remain inadequate without their help. You internalize that dynamic: the feeling of not being enough, of needing more content, more sessions, more external guidance. This makes it harder to trust your judgment, your instincts, and your ability to move forward without instructions.

The most severe damage is not the money or time lost. It is the internal sabotage. The guru's voice, full of certainties, settles in your mind and takes the place of your own. You become dependent on that "external reading," because your own voice—fainter and more hesitant—feels like interference. You begin consulting them about everything before acting, as if your inner self needed permission. If your intuition tells you, “This doesn't feel right," but the guru tells you, "This is part of your resistance" or "these are your limiting beliefs," you learn to distrust yourself. You choose external certainty over your inner truth.

That is the real break—not the one you had at the beginning, but the one caused by the savior.

What no guru will say, because it destroys their model, is that you already have everything you need. You are not broken or incomplete, and you do not need to be saved. You go through periods of confusion, exhaustion, and loss. That does not make you deficient; it simply means you are human.

The distinction lies between those who recognize your strength and support you as it unfolds, and those who benefit from keeping you convinced that you cannot do without them. One recognizes your self-authority as ultimate and inherent; the other fragments it to turn your dependence into a business model.

How much longer are you going to keep looking outside for what you already know is taking shape within you?

Genuine respect does not come wrapped in infallible formulas or promises of immediate change. It does not set the pace for you or decide for you. It observes, shares, and trusts that you will know what to do with what you receive.

What power do you give away when you allow others to direct your life? What do you lose when you hand over control?

Giving up that weight does not free you; it strips you of your authority. Where your responsibility goes, your capacity to transform things goes with it.

Real growth does not happen under the guidance of someone who feeds on your dependence. It happens when you recognize that no one has the answers to your life—because no one else lives it—and you stop looking for saviors and start trusting yourself, even when the horizon becomes unclear.

Then the guru disappears, and only your voice remains. When the guru disappears, how willing are you to endure the vertigo of listening to yourself?

Every time you don't decide, someone else does it for you.

CHAPTER 2: The Cost of Not Choosing

Every time you don't decide, someone else does it for you. Are you comfortable giving up your right to choose?

You haven't responded to that email in weeks because you don't know what to say; the relationship you can't seem to start or end remains in limbo; the project you wanted to begin has been sitting in the "someday" folder for months, gathering digital dust. The conversation you've been avoiding because it might make someone else uncomfortable continues to burn inside you.

All these omissions weigh on us. What weighs us down, like a backpack full of stones, is what we haven't experienced, felt, or lived—not the mistakes themselves. Every time you postpone a decision that you know is yours to make, you are not only delaying an outcome but also handing over a part of your life to someone else.

There is an almost imperceptible way of surrendering your decision-making power. Others don't take it from you—you give it away. You wait, you procrastinate, and you let time choose for you. And we know that time has no judgment; it simply moves forward. You end up with relationships that grow cold, paths that close, and opportunities that pass you by without waiting. On the surface, you remain still—but inside, something is quietly fading.

You feel a kind of exhaustion that doesn't come from overexertion, but from the accumulation of what you haven't done—from asking yourself, "what would have happened if…?" It's the wear and tear of maintaining silent truces, of holding back movement, of pausing the words you wanted to say. Over time, this accumulation becomes a burden that even rest cannot repair. It is the fatigue of carrying what you didn't dare to decide.

What decision have you been avoiding for so long that you no longer even mention it to yourself?

There are two main ways we avoid making decisions—each with its own disguise.

The first is fear: fear of making a mistake, of being judged, of losing something, of everything collapsing if you take a step. Fear has many faces. Sometimes it appears as caution, sometimes as excessive calculation, and other times as the need for more information that you can't actually obtain. If you don't recognize it, it operates in the shadows and paralyzes you.

The second form is more subtle: waiting for "the perfect moment." As if there were a crystal ball that could tell you when the conditions will finally be right.

This waiting sounds reasonable—even responsible: "I'm not ready yet," "I need more information," "I'll act when I have a clearer picture." But clarity doesn't come from thinking alone; it comes from acting. When you act, the context responds and gives you feedback you couldn't have seen before.

Patience, however, is something else entirely. Patience pauses because something needs time to mature; procrastination delays because you're afraid to move. Calling paralysis "prudence" is more common than we like to admit.

What decision have you postponed by calling it "prudence" when it was really fear?

Not all waiting is the same. Bread dough needs time to rise. If you take it out too early, you ruin it; if you leave it too long, you ruin it too. Some processes have their own timing—forcing them destroys them. Patience is knowing how to wait.

Now imagine this: the bus is coming. You see it approaching. Your instinct says, "Now." But you hesitate. "Should I get on? Is it the right one? What if it takes me somewhere else?" While you hesitate, it passes. You missed it—not because you weren't ready, but because you didn't act at the right moment.

The third form—and the most common—is waiting for things to resolve themselves. Hoping a relationship will fix itself without conversation, that a project will write itself without effort, that life will change without you changing anything. In this case, you're not letting something mature—you're using waiting as an excuse not to move.

Many people confuse these three: they rush what requires time, delay what won't resolve on its own, or let opportunities pass out of insecurity.

The difference doesn't come from outside. It comes from within—and it's called discernment. Discernment is not something you either have or don't; it is developed by honestly examining your own decisions, without embellishing or justifying them.

The signs are not in your head—they are within you. When waiting is right, there is calm; something matures, and you know it without tension. When action is needed, your instinct pushes you forward—you feel that if you don't act now, something will slip away.

When you delay out of fear, tension builds. You become restless, distracted. You check your phone, open random tabs, do anything except what you know matters.

The difference is tangible—you can't think your way out of it. Deep down, you already know when to wait and when to act. You just must pay attention and listen to yourself.

There will be moments when loneliness feels so heavy that any strong external voice seems like a lifeline.

It's easy to cling to someone who speaks with certainty, as if their answer were salvation. So, ask yourself: what do you feel when you accept a belief that has no real foundation?

What happens inside you when you surrender your will to an idea that leaves no room for doubt—just because that voice sounded stronger than yours?

You don't have to answer right away. Just let the question linger.

The greatest risk is forgetting your own voice. Outside, there will always be louder voices, stronger narratives, promises of certainty. Amid all that noise, yours may sound like a whisper. But it's there—waiting for space.

What would happen if, instead of chasing what others claim is true, you stopped to listen to what is insistently emerging within you?

What would you discover if you stopped repeating other people's words and started speaking your own?

Listening too closely to external voices carries a risk. It's like driving while letting go of the wheel to join a conversation in the back seat—you already know how that ends. The same happens in life when you abandon your direction to follow external noise: the path ends up being set without you.

We live in a time that seems ideal for independent thinking. Never before has access to information been so widespread. You no longer need formal credentials to learn, nor intermediaries to interpret reality. And yet, never has blind obedience been so normalized—as if all that access existed not to think, but to avoid thinking, to reinforce the comfort of being told how to live.

Information is everywhere. Wisdom is built within. So what is the point of living with the security of obedience, if in the end you follow paths you've never even questioned?

Have you caught yourself looking sideways at someone else's life, measuring yours against theirs?

Beneath this lies a deeper tension—a voice that constantly says: "Me." The need to be right, to convince, to turn every word into performance.

You notice it when what you do loses value unless it's recognized, when you speak to persuade rather than to communicate, when your worth depends on being seen.

What do you gain from believing you hold absolute truth? Are there rewards for living that way? No medals, no trophies for being louder or more certain.

What situation in your life is trying to tell you something your mind refuses to hear?

Think about the last times you acted. Something happened—it went well or badly—but you learned something. You either regretted it or were glad you acted. Every one of those experiences left a mark.

Now think about the times you waited. Sometimes waiting was right and something matured. Other times, you simply let time pass—and the opportunity disappeared. Like missing the bus. You saw it, hesitated, and it was gone.

Something held you back—likely fear, or a lack of information that seemed reasonable at the time but later revealed itself as an excuse.

What did you learn the last time you let an opportunity pass?

Discernment sharpens with every conscious decision: when you move forward despite uncertainty; when you choose to wait despite external pressure; when you recognize, "this was fear—not prudence," and accept it honestly.

You already know when to act and when to wait. It's your mind that confuses you.

Your life decisions are yours. But if you don't distinguish between action and inaction, you end up choosing from fear or habit—and both lead to the same place: a place that doesn't belong to you.

The real burden of not choosing fractures your inner self. Every time you delegate a decision, something inside you goes silent. It doesn't protest—it just fades.

What's at stake is not just opportunity, but your relationship with yourself.

Eventually, everything catches up. What you feared losing is lost—because you didn't act. What you hoped would resolve itself didn't. The bus you once saw coming no longer stops at your corner.

Life doesn't pause. Every space you leave empty will be filled. Every decision you avoid will be made—by something or someone else. And what disappears is not only opportunity, but the possibility of things ever being the way they once were.

Even if choosing doesn't give you certainty, it gives you direction. And direction—no matter how often corrected—moves you out of stagnation.

There is a decision in front of you right now. You can feel it. Maybe it's time to let something mature. Maybe it's time to act. Or maybe it's time to stop hiding behind waiting.

Only you know.

What once controlled you now has a name. And what has a name can be worked with.

CHAPTER 3: The Underlying Forces

This is not a lack of judgment; it usually revolves around old habits, entrenched loyalties, and unresolved elements from the past that still carry weight in the present. They were formed in response to contexts that once protected you and served a purpose. Today, they hinder more than they help.

When you understand what is limiting your ability to decide, these imprints begin to lose their power. Becoming aware of these patterns requires discernment—and the willingness to set aside blame. They may not disappear immediately, but they stop operating in the shadows. They are responses that once made sense, even if today you confuse them with personality traits or flaws. Many are outdated; others are simply defense mechanisms that no longer serve you.

Here are some of the most common patterns. You may recognize yourself in one or more of them. It happens to almost all of us. By identifying them, you can begin to stop obeying them.

External pressure: The fear of disappointing others

As a child, you learned a basic rule: acceptance ensured care. When you met expectations, you received approval, attention, and security. That rule was useful—it kept you connected to those you depended on. The problem arises when that mechanism persists into adulthood as if it were still necessary.

Therefore, you begin to orient your choices around the approval of others. You measure what you say, you edit what you do. You calculate reactions and surrender your judgment to standards you never chose. It often goes unnoticed because it operates subtly.

You see it in everyday concessions: the degree you pursued because your family expected it; the job you accepted because it "looked good" on your résumé; the relationship you stayed in longer than you should have because ending it would have disappointed others.

This constant vigilance is exhausting. Every decision is filtered first through "what will they think?" and only afterward through "what do I want?" Over time, it becomes difficult to distinguish between your own will and what you believe you should want. At its core lies the fear of disappointing others.

What part of you hides behind the need to please—and what do you fear would happen if you stopped?

Other people's scripts: The maps you didn't draw

From an early age, you received an implicit—but very clear—model of what a "successful" life looks like: pursue a certain career, achieve visible milestones, build a relationship, acquire assets. The specifics vary depending on context, but the pressure is the same: follow the script.

Often, beneath this are your parents' unfulfilled ambitions. A mother who wanted to be a doctor pushes you toward achievement; a father who feared instability instills in you a deep aversion to risk. These influences are not necessarily intentional—they arise from unresolved experiences.

The same dynamic appears at a systemic level. You are rewarded for productivity and penalized for inactivity. You are measured by externals: what you have, what you produce, what you accumulate. And it is reinforced by what you consume: curated success, edited realities, narratives designed to persuade.

You postpone your personal life until you "fulfill" external expectations. But that demand is never satisfied—because there is always another goal, another standard.

What are you pursuing today that genuinely comes from you? And to what extent is it an inherited script you never questioned?

Which part of that script would you rewrite first?

Internal dialogue: The narratives that define you

Your mind has a voice—and it speaks constantly. Many of its statements are not facts, but inherited interpretations disguised as truths: "I always give up," "I'm not good at public speaking," "I never succeed."

These statements are not reality—they are conclusions drawn from earlier experiences that were never fully processed. You were told you lacked discipline, and you accepted it. Now you abandon projects halfway through—not because you lack commitment, but because you believe that's who you are.

These narratives become self-fulfilling. You act in ways that reinforce them.

And they're not always negative. Even positive identities can limit you: "I'm the responsible one," "I solve everything," "I'm the strong one." When these labels become rigid, they prevent you from exploring other aspects of yourself.

You dismiss feedback that contradicts them. If you believe "I'm not good at sales" and someone recognizes your ability to communicate, you disregard it. If an opportunity doesn't fit your identity, you reject it. Turning a feeling into an identity traps you.

Which label have you been using as an excuse not to change—and what would happen if you let it go?

The weight of past experiences: The past, still active

Some experiences remain active long after they've passed. A conflict that was never resolved. A comment that stayed with you. A moment when you felt exposed or dismissed. These memories become reference points. They act like invisible anchors.

A colleague once mocked how you spoke. An idea you shared was dismissed. You were open, and the other person withdrew. These moments become amplified in memory.

Today, they influence your behavior in situations that are no longer the same. You avoid speaking up because you once stayed silent. You avoid intimacy because you were once hurt.

The problem arises when a past event becomes a rule: "It happened once—it will happen again." Each time it resurfaces, you react as if it were happening now.

What past experience continues to shape your present decisions, even though the context has changed?

Safe territory: Attachment to the familiar

This pattern appears as a preference for what is known. Familiar environments, routines, and relationships provide a sense of control. You know what to expect—there are no surprises.

But that sense of stability has a cost: it limits your experience. You stop exploring because you believe you already know what you like. You confuse familiarity with satisfaction. You say, "This is just who I am," when what you really mean is, "This is what I know."

Those are not the same.

What routine, relationship, or environment are you maintaining simply because it is familiar—even though it no longer adds anything to your life?

Environment and energy: The people around you

The people around you matter—not just as contacts, but as sources of energy. Some amplify problems without offering perspective. They criticize without contributing. They require constant adaptation from you. Often, they operate from their own fears and project them outward. They need you to stay the same so they can feel comfortable.

Being around people who question your decisions or diminish your progress drains your confidence.

You may have shared an idea or project with enthusiasm—only to be met with judgment or unsolicited advice. Understanding that they speak from their own limitations prevents resentment. But continuing to adapt yourself to maintain that dynamic drains the energy you need to move forward.

Who do you feel depleted after spending time with—even if the interaction seems harmless?

Lack of internal drive: The engine turned off

The energy required for change comes from within—not from external expectations. When you are disconnected from what moves you, everything becomes mechanical. You act out of obligation, not intention. Any difficulty becomes a reason to stop.

Reconnecting requires space. It requires slowing down enough to listen to what genuinely moves you—and allowing yourself to explore it, even without certainty.

When you begin to name these patterns, they start to lose their power. The next time they appear, you will recognize them instead of mistaking them for who you are.

What once controlled you now has a name. And what has a name can be worked with.

Now that you can see these underlying forces—will you continue to let them decide for you, or will you confront them?

Transformation begins with a precise understanding of where you are—not where you imagine yourself to be.

CHAPTER 4: Understanding Where You Are

What are you doing with your existence today? I am not asking you in general or philosophical terms; I am asking you about today, this week, this month. If someone were to examine your last seven days as an auditor reviews a statement of account, what would they find? Would that cold record match what you say matters to you, or would it reveal a completely different story?

It is much easier to talk about abstract goals than to analyze the reality of everyday life. While you construct narratives about who you are, the days pass—and what you actually did with them is the only thing that can be verified. That record reveals what remained at the end of the day, what or who you paid attention to, and how much space was given to what you claim to value.

What does your inventory reveal about the gap between what you say and what you do?

You simply have to acknowledge it. While you build complex explanations or justify delays, time continues to pass without asking for permission. A small adjustment in a single decision can begin to shift everything. Observing yourself honestly helps you regain order—even when you don't like what you see.

What have you been avoiding seeing, and what would it reveal if you used it as a reference point?

Here, we are talking about an inventory of facts—not theory: a kind of forensic review of how your time was spent, with what justifications and with what consequences. You may claim to value your health, your relationships, or your clarity—but those are measured through action, through where you place your attention. The contrast is simple: your actions either align with your words or contradict them.

Admitting things as they are, without embellishment, immediately shifts the position from which you make decisions.

Look at the past few days and ask yourself: what did you spend most of your time on? How much of that reflects what you say matters to you? What did you say yes to this week, knowing you didn't want to—and what did it cost you? Has what is central to your life had a real place in your schedule, or does it exist only in your imagination?

It's enough to recall where you were, what you did, who you spoke to, and what occupied your attention—you don't need a perfect record. If you can't answer this concretely, you already have your first clue: what filled your day didn't leave enough of an impression to be remembered.

This happens when you live on autopilot—like someone driving a familiar route and arriving without remembering the journey. The day fills with movement, but not direction. Urgent tasks are completed, but what is essential remains untouched. In the end, busyness is mistaken for progress.

There is often a gap—sometimes a wide one—between what you say you value and how you use your time. This gap is not always hypocrisy; more often, it is habit. Decisions made years ago continue to consume your present: the job you took "temporarily" and have held for years, the routine that no longer serves you but persists, the relationship that neither evolves nor ends.

The problem is not the gap—it is failing to see it. As long as it remains invisible, you will continue believing that you "don't have time" for what matters, when in reality, your time is already occupied by something else that, deep down, doesn't matter to you.

Your energy is also part of the inventory. Every activity has a cost. Some things drain you emotionally, even when they require little effort; others exhaust you physically but leave you restored. Like going to the gym—you come back tired, but restored. The difference is not in the effort, but in alignment. What you choose can be recovered; what you endure accumulates.

You can review recent days and ask yourself what left you most depleted—not in terms of effort, but in terms of meaning. The meeting you knew was pointless. The conversation that went nowhere. The commitment you accepted without interest. The list can be long.

Every time you invest energy in something meaningless, that energy is gone. Not dramatically—but steadily.

Your body is part of this inventory. Tension in your shoulders, shallow breathing, clenched teeth—these are not coincidences. They are signals. If your schedule suggests everything is fine, but your body tells a different story, pay attention to the body. It reflects what you are sustaining.

Irritability, interrupted sleep, disproportionate reactions—none of this is random. It points to something you are not addressing. That fatigue is not from doing too much, but from living in a way that no longer fits.

The signals are there. The question is whether you notice them—or explain them away.

You will likely see things you would prefer not to see. You may realize that what you claim to value is not reflected in your actions, that you maintain empty routines, that you invest your time in situations that give nothing back. That discomfort is not a problem—it is evidence that you are actually looking.

The first impulse will be to justify yourself: "I didn't have time," "it was an unusual week." That may be true—but it may also be the most refined way of avoiding reality. The goal is not to judge yourself, but to obtain clear, usable data.

Without that, any attempt at change is built on distortion. Transformation begins with a precise understanding of where you are—not where you imagine yourself to be.

Rather than trying to fix everything at once, the task is simpler: define your starting point with clarity. This is where I am. This is what I am doing. This is how I feel.

From there, everything else becomes possible.

Resignation is the end of the road. Acceptance is the beginning.

CHAPTER 5: Accepting Versus Resigning

You have finished examining your life without mercy; you have taken stock of events and seen the gap between what you say you value and what you do with your time. Now, with that information on the table, you face the most decisive question of all: What are you going to do with what you have seen?

Most people give up at this point without even realizing it, falling into the most common trap in personal development: confusing acceptance with resignation.

Resignation is giving up. It is an internal stance with many forms. You can recognize it as paralysis disguised as realism: you convince yourself that "that's just the way things are," and that being pragmatic means giving up trying—when in reality, you are justifying your immobility.

This attitude leads to a complete loss of agency. You stop being the central actor in your own life and become a passive spectator who only absorbs impact, convinced that you have no influence over the outcome. What makes it harmful is that it normalizes discomfort; you become accustomed to confusion, disrespect, or lack of direction, just as one grows accustomed to a persistent irritation.

The internal cost can be devastating. Resignation erodes self-esteem; every day you tolerate what you don't want, you reinforce the idea that you don't deserve better. To endure it, you develop a form of emotional anesthesia: you numb yourself just enough to avoid pain—but in doing so, you also lose access to enthusiasm and joy. Gradually, you shut down.

The final consequence is a narrowing of possibilities. By assuming nothing can change, you stop noticing what could. And within that confinement, a quiet resentment grows—a bitterness that may not explode, but slowly corrodes your relationships and your character, turning you cynical and detached.

Acceptance, by contrast, operates in the opposite direction. Resignation paralyzes; acceptance restores movement. It pulls you out of mental stagnation and allows you to take the next step. It reestablishes agency and responsibility, reminding you that you always retain a degree of control over how you respond.

Rather than dragging you down, acceptance clarifies your self-perception because you stop deceiving yourself. Instead of minimizing or avoiding discomfort, you name it directly—and in doing so, you transform it from something diffuse into something you can address.

This clarity expands your perspective. You begin to notice openings where before you saw only obstacles. It becomes a process that transforms accumulated frustration into direction.

The distinction between the two is subtle but decisive. Resignation assumes everything is fixed. Acceptance rests on the ability to recognize what cannot be changed—and the willingness to act on what can.

The phrase "When life gives you lemons, make lemonade" is often used to illustrate this idea. It involves recognizing the lemon (what is outside your control) and making lemonade (what you can do in response).

Confusing acceptance with tolerance is a serious mistake. Tolerating abuse, injustice, or disrespect belongs to resignation. You might remain in a difficult job by consciously choosing to stay while you look for alternatives—that is acceptance. Remaining there convinced that you "have no way out," repeating that "it is what it is" while you fade, is resignation.

True acceptance is the starting point of change. Fully acknowledging that something is harmful, unfair, or no longer right for you is what allows you to gather the energy to move away from it. Change begins with recognition.

The greatest risk is using the language of acceptance to justify inaction. If, beneath the surface, you are still waiting for reality to shift without your involvement, you remain trapped. If what you call acceptance leaves behind resentment, complaint, or bitterness, then it is not acceptance—it is surrender.

In what area of your life have you been using the language of acceptance to justify resignation?

What are you calling "something I can't change" that you are, in fact, avoiding?

What would happen if, instead of resigning yourself, you accepted it as a starting point and chose to act?

Resignation is the end of the road. Acceptance is the beginning.

In what areas have you resigned yourself by calling it acceptance, and what would you do differently if you chose to accept, take responsibility, and act?

The time you spend validating the lives of other people is time you do not spend living your own.

CHAPTER 6: The Power of Your Attention

After you closed the door, the day fell apart into tiny fragments. You answered messages, opened documents, responded to various voices, and jumped between windows as quickly as you would change lanes while driving. Despite all the movement, it is difficult to pinpoint what remained steady.

There is no need to look for someone to blame or to exaggerate; we must simply recognize a physical fact: fragmented attention brings only the surface of experience into view. The nuance is clear: digging a deep hole in a small area finds water; making a hundred shallow holes in the ground only raises dust.

Being truly present shapes what takes root in daily life. Constant activity often lacks concrete progress. Attending to the urgent, responding to the immediate, and starting from the beginning again without anything changing creates a mirage of productivity. That constant movement simulates progress, but nothing actually advances.

Every interruption has a price that you rarely measure: the time it takes to get back on track, the energy required to begin again, and the patience needed to pick up where you left off. That cost explains the feeling of having done a great deal and still remained in the same place. It is the exhaustion of having gone in circles for eight hours instead of moving toward what matters.

What would have been different if you had protected a block of time and left behind something tangible?

Your focus is like a beam of light. Where it falls, the edges are defined; where it recedes, everything dissolves into darkness. If you move it constantly, nothing takes shape; if you keep it fixed, a recognizable figure emerges, and you can make informed choices.

Attention goes beyond productivity; it is the prerequisite for everything else. Without it, nothing leaves a lasting trace.

Internal signals pass by because no one is observing; the body speaks, but its messages are lost in the interference of constant movement. What you feel, what bothers you, what attracts you—all of this requires a brief pause to be perceived. When that pause does not exist, you live responding without knowing to what, acting without truly choosing, moving forward without direction of your own. The day passes, and you barely notice it.

There is also no real distinction: you cannot separate what you want from what you were taught to want if you never stop to listen to yourself. The voice from outside and the voice from within end up sounding the same, and you obey without knowing which one you are following. That confusion is resolved by being present.

Without focus, authority is ineffective; discernment is the technical requirement for exercising command.

Attention is the muscle that drives the entire process. Without it, nothing that comes after can be of any use.

Today, few things capture our attention as effectively as screens. The problem lies in using them indiscriminately, letting them decide for you what, when, and who deserves your focus. Constant comparison on social media embodies the most modern way to squander your concentration. It is a waste of time designed to keep you scrolling endlessly and consuming the "perfection of others" while your own situation becomes increasingly blurred.

When your attention is captured by the outside world, you fall into the most sophisticated way of avoiding your own decisions: competition. That invisible race to prove who knows more, who has more, who does it better, who runs faster, who gets there first. Mine versus yours. This obsession with comparing ourselves robs us of peace of mind and drags us toward what doesn't matter.

It works just like the guru's dynamic, but in daily doses, like a hypnotic act. Look at your fingers. Watch them as you automatically swipe through screens, as if even your fingerprints were being worn away. You see a stranger's tidy house, a colleague's financial success, or a couple's ideal trip, and suddenly your immediate surroundings seem inadequate.

And what remains afterward? Is it frustration, envy, resentment, or the feeling of being less than?

We seek distraction, escape, evasion; we flee into a digital anesthesia that robs us of our real experience. We are avoiding tranquility. We ignore the gap between what we have and what we would like to have.

Sometimes it isn't even jealousy; it's boredom. But that entertainment comes at a real cost. The time you spend validating the lives of other people is time you do not spend living your own. It is like watching a race from the stands: you watch others run toward paradise, analyze their steps, and see them cross the finish line. When the event ends and you are still in the same seat, complaining loses its logic. There was no external impediment; between consuming the lives of others and living your own, the choice was to remain a spectator.

Determining where the beam of light falls restores your hours to their proper shape. What needs definition today gets it until there is no trace left; the rest waits without drama. When this discipline takes hold, the day ceases to resemble a catalog of open windows and regains its structure.

A sustained activity has a beginning, middle, and end. Rather than demanding perfection, it requires ending the day on a firm note. That ending reduces tension, avoids constant restarts, and curbs the compulsion to take on too much and accomplish too little.

Presence and continuity allow you to see what you previously missed. When you are scattered, you react to the immediate and confuse volume with value; with continuity, nuances emerge, your judgment becomes more refined, and you make wiser decisions.

Hidden costs accumulate when you slow down and start up again without pause. That is why some days end calmly because there was substance, and others demand external stimuli to hide the discomfort of having been nothing more than a sum of disconnected parts.

Like a carpenter adjusting the level on a board, your focus will wander. It's inevitable. The goal is to notice when the bubble shifts and simply return it to the center, with the firmness of someone correcting the course of the steering wheel.

How many times this week did your focus get lost in the trivial, and how hard was it for you to admit it?

That is the power of your attention: noticing when it wanders and readjusting it. Each intentional adjustment strengthens the muscle that holds on to what is important.

The next time you find yourself rushing, will you be able to stop and ask yourself what you want to see, or will you keep spinning without ever really looking?

Copying someone else's path is like building on a foundation that was never yours. Eventually, it collapses.

CHAPTER 7: The Fallacy Of "If I Can Do It, So Can You"

"If I can do it, so can you." The phrase sounds motivating and inspiring, full of possibility. It is repeated on social media, in books, and at conferences. And every time we hear it, something inside us is triggered: that mixture of hope and pressure, of possibility and guilt. The implicit doubt is devastating: If they could do it, why can't you?

We say it with good intentions, seeking to encourage. Even so, the premise is incomplete. That phrase assumes that the conditions under which someone achieved something can be replicated. In some specific cases, this is true—but in most, it is a trap.

If someone says to you, "I assembled this shelf by following the instructions—you can do it," the statement makes sense. Assembling furniture with instructions is a mechanical process where the variables are controlled. If you have the same parts and follow the same steps, you will achieve the same result. In that scenario, "if I can do it, you can do it" retains its validity.

Building a career, strengthening a relationship, or recovering from a loss belong to a completely different category. These processes come without an instruction manual and without interchangeable parts. The variables are endless, many are beyond your control, and what worked for someone in certain conditions can fail entirely in another context.

It would be absurd to imagine an established painter saying to a beginner, "If I made it into museums, so can you." That statement sounds illogical in such a different context. Yet we accept that logic when the differences are less visible: start-up capital, networks, emotional stability, access to education, mental health, and the margin for error that your situation allows.

Growing up with parents who validated emotions provides a completely different foundation than growing up in an environment where feelings had to be hidden. Borrowing money from your family creates a different sense of security than having no financial support network. Pretending that these differences do not exist—and that we all start from the same point with the same tools—is a form of self-deception.

The culture of success promotes the idea that achievements are solely the result of individual effort. It offers packaged models: the habits of millionaires, the routines of successful entrepreneurs, the steps of influencers. The promise is tempting: "Follow them, and you will reach the same destination."

What is deliberately omitted is who financed the early stages, who assumed the risks, what connections were inherited, and under what economic conditions the process unfolded. These details are excluded because they disrupt the narrative. Without them, the story stops being useful information and becomes motivational fiction.

Role models can serve as reference points. Seeing how someone overcame a challenge may offer insight and perspective. But what worked in their specific circumstances must be translated into your own context.

Copying without considering context guarantees frustration. Every method you try and abandon adds to an internal record of failure. Over time, doubt shifts from the method to yourself. The narrative changes from "this didn't work" to "I am the one who doesn't work." From that moment on, each new attempt carries the accumulated weight of all previous ones.

Your mind registers that mismatch. The anxiety of not being where you believe you should be—and the tension that arises when comparing your path to someone else's—creates a constant sense of inadequacy.

What part of yourself have you ignored while trying to fit into someone else's model of success?

Recognizing this is the first step toward building from your own ground. No one tells you this because it doesn't sell: your path is not transferable. You can learn from others, observe what they did, and test what might be useful. That is translation.

If someone left a stable job to start a business, observe how they handled uncertainty, what trade-offs they accepted, and what conditions made it possible. That is useful. Quitting your job tomorrow just because it worked for them is not strategy—it is imitation.

Translation requires knowing your resources, your constraints, and your starting point. It demands honesty: what applies, what does not, and what must be adapted.

Copying someone else's path is like building on a foundation that was never yours. Eventually, it collapses.

When it does, you have two options: blame yourself for not being able to sustain it, or recognize that it was never designed for you. That realization breaks the cycle of self-blame and redirects attention to the real issue—the foundation.

At that point, you stop asking which path worked for someone else and begin asking what direction makes sense for you, from where you are, with what you have.

Understanding that your path is unique can feel unsettling. There is no template, no guarantee, no familiar narrative to follow. It may not inspire others. It may not even look impressive.

But it will be yours.

Does that unsettle you—or does it free you?

The discomfort signals the loss of external reference. The relief reveals that the weight of comparison has lifted. What remains is a space where no one else will step in to decide for you.

Because this is the point where guidance ends—and choice begins.

Section 2 - The RADIAR Process

A map raises questions and shows you the terrain so you can decide where to walk.

CHAPTER 8: RADIAR

It's normal at this point to be thinking, "You just spent an entire chapter criticizing gurus who sell foolproof methods—and now you're going to present me with yours?"

You are right to be skeptical.

The criticism in the opening chapter was aimed at dogma—rigid formulas that promise to save you in exchange for obedience. What you have before you is a map.

There is a key distinction: dogma provides closed answers and demands submission; a map raises questions and shows you the terrain so you can decide where to walk.

RADIAR's sole purpose is to restore the authority you have ceded to others. This process is designed to help you stop following external instructions and start listening to yourself.

It is a structure of questions that functions as a mirror. I do not have your answers. The work, the decisions, and the power have been and remain yours. This structure exists only to remind you that you can use it in your own way and go wherever you choose.

Most models of personal transformation promise a linear path; you start at point A, follow defined steps, and arrive at point B. That straight line is often a dead end because it conceals the true horizon. In RADIAR, the present is the landscape.

It works on a different logic. Instead of taking you to an end point, it brings you back to yourself again and again, from a clearer level of understanding each time. Arriving at a new form requires observing yourself in successive cycles until the rough edges soften. Each iteration seems to return you to the same place, but the perspective shifts; you are at a higher vantage point, with greater clarity. The essential thing is to recognize that each return to yourself reveals a new layer.

Think of a rock on the seashore. The rock is redefined by the constant return of the waves, not by a single impact. Each wave returns and hits it; the rock does not flee; it remains and its edges are worn down over time. The sea subjects it to a relentless flow. In the end, the stone has lost its points of resistance. It is smoother, simpler, and aligned with its own structure.

This is how RADIAR operates. Reality is a constant flow, and your ability to return to the sequence allows you to release rigidity. In that inevitable friction, your essence is revealed without being distorted. Repetition refines. Accepting that the path may be uneven partly removes the obsession with arriving. Here we pursue the willingness to return differently each time, not a perfect and static state.

RADIAR is born from concrete experience. Reading these pages straight through will not be enough. Authentic transformation happens through concrete actions: the limits you set, the words you choose to keep silent or to speak, the decision you have been putting off. This is effective when done with awareness, honesty, and calm.

The process is activated in those daily moments when no one applauds, but when everything is defined. In those moments, theory becomes reality.

This practice has structure. RADIAR consists of six sequential stages. The order ensures that each movement prepares the ground for the next. What once seemed obvious to you may challenge you in another phase. The essence of the sequence deepens with each repetition. Each return brings with it the possibility of greater understanding.

The essential happens in private, and that inner work inevitably filters outward. It shows in the way you respond, how you choose to relate, and what you decide to support. Your actions become the evidence.

RADIAR creates an open space. You return to the tool because a new situation calls for a new adjustment. That openness to transition allows you to recalibrate your point of reference. The value of the guide lies in reminding you that you choose the direction.

We live in an era that idolizes the immediate; RADIAR insists on circularity, proposing pauses and new beginnings if necessary or if you want to tackle something different. The brain learns in stages. Consolidation comes with return.

The name is no coincidence. RADIAR comes from the initials of each stage: Rediscovery, Authenticity, Deployment, Integration, Action, Reaffirmation. The entire process fits into a single word that you can carry with you.

RADIAR has no graduation or certificates. The only thing that changes is the way you see yourself, the way you make decisions, and the mark you leave on your environment.

Its power lies in freeing you from competition and comparison.

Verification will be simple: What has changed in you? What decision have you stopped postponing? What relationship has become clearer? What internal space have you reclaimed? Your reality is the only evidence.

Are you willing to face what you have hidden even from yourself, to see the scene you have been avoiding, and to discover what could come out of it if you confront it?

RADIAR on a page

The anxious reader changes the object. What they avoid is not the book: it is the evidence within.

Use this page as a reminder, not as a requirement. If you want to quickly review the itinerary, come back to it. It is for when you feel like you have lost your way or when you want to see the six stages at a glance before starting a new sequence.

The progression is cyclical, not linear. Return to yourself at each turn:

1. **Rediscovery**: Who are you without the persona you represent? What do you want in your life?
2. **Authenticity**: How do you live as that person?
3. **Deployment**: Translate your truth into one minimal, verifiable action.

4. **Integration**: Let what you have done take its place.

5. **Action**: Move something in your chosen direction.

6. **Reaffirmation**: Hold on to what serves you, let go of what does not.

The cycle does not end; it returns with increasing clarity.

How to use it

The first cycle begins, without exception, with Rediscovery (1). First, you need to see where you are, what life you are living, and what patterns you are repeating before moving forward.

Then you move forward in order: Authenticity (2), Deployment (3), Integration (4), Action (5), and Reaffirmation (6). It makes no sense to jump from one stage to another depending on your state of mind; the sequence supports coherence.

In the following stages, if in Action (5) you notice that something doesn't fit, don't suddenly go back to the beginning. First, return to Integration (4) to check if the new element has a real place in your life. If it still doesn't fit, you can go back to Deployment (3) to adjust the minimal action and, from there, resume the sequence.

The sequence matters. Returning refines the process so that what you build makes sense to you.

Visualize it this way: suppose there is something you say matters to you and it is not on your agenda. With RADIAR, you first look honestly at what you are doing and what you really want (Rediscovery). Then, you check whether your current way of living matches who you say you are (Authenticity). From there, you choose a minimal, concrete action that reflects it (Deployment) and make space for it in your life, adjusting what is necessary (Integration). Then you move something in the structure, not just the detail (Action). Finally, you decide what stays, what you let go of, and what you adjust for the next sequence (Reaffirmation).

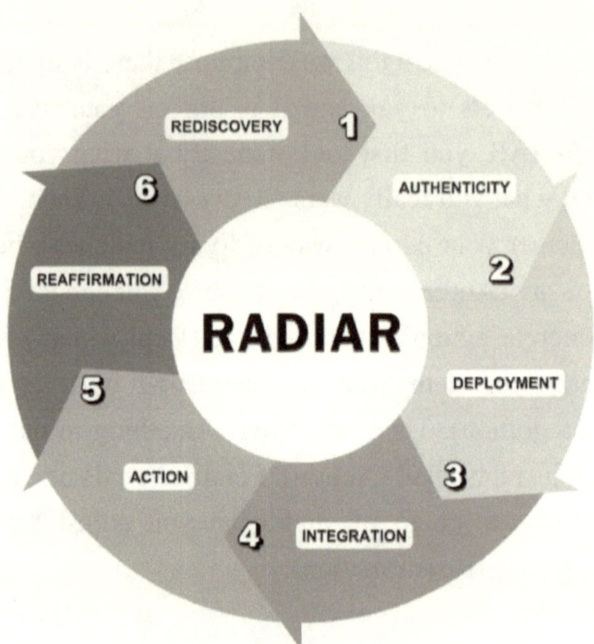

The process never ends. Come back.

What you face can be managed. What you avoid will continue to operate in the background.

CHAPTER 9: Stage 1- Rediscovery

Who are you?

I am not referring to the version you show in public or the role you skillfully play to keep the peace. I am not talking about the polished story you tell when someone asks you what you do for a living. I am talking about who you are when no one is looking.

What do you want?

What does that voice you hear when you're alone—the one that's sometimes hard to put into words—tell you? It tells you that you'd rather be somewhere else, doing something else, or being someone else. It's the voice that speaks when the protagonist has no audience.

I know this is a difficult question to address because it is hard to answer with facts. You have spent years building an acceptable "version" of yourself, tailored to what was expected: the responsible son, the efficient employee, the understanding partner, the friend who is always available. Each role has its facade. You follow it smoothly and it works—until you start to feel a warning sign that is difficult to explain. It is the feeling of performing a life instead of living it.

You respond as you are supposed to respond and choose what you are supposed to choose. In the end, it is difficult to see what is truly yours and what is mechanical. You can start by recognizing whether much of what you do, think, and maintain comes from you or was inherited and carried without question.

To see this clearly, I suggest an exercise in radical honesty. What has occupied your attention today can be divided into two columns.

The first column is what depended on you: your decisions, your responses, and your way of interpreting what happened. The second column is what did not depend on you: other people's opinions, the final result, the past, the weather, other people's choices.

If you like, take a sheet of paper. In the first column, write down what was in your hands today. For example: "I decided not to reply to that message until I had things clear in my mind," "I chose to go for a walk instead of going over the same issue again and again," "I responded calmly even though I was provoked." In the second column, write down what was beyond your control: "My boss changing his mind," "her understanding what I meant," "the outcome of the interview," "what happened yesterday."

If you find that you have devoted more than half of your energy to the second column, you have found the source of your exhaustion. It is not effort—it is misdirected effort. You tried to move what cannot be moved by your effort or your will.

The boundary between the two columns is invisible but precise. Crossing it without realizing it is more exhausting than any physical effort. What does not depend on you has no solution in that moment. If it's pouring rain and you don't have a roof, there will be no party; regretting it won't stop the rain, nor will complaining build a roof. Regretting what you could have done yesterday doesn't change today either. What remains is to move on, learn from what happened, and focus on what is possible.

On the side of what you cannot control, there is only room for acceptance: it is what it is. On the side of what you can control, there is decision. Mixing them guarantees stagnation.

How have you wasted your personal energy today trying to change things that were not up to you?

What decision within your sphere of control have you avoided because you were focused on the external?

That recurring thought often appears: "I'm not going to be able to handle this." It feels convincing. But that thought is just a mental event—not a truth. And just as it appeared, it can disappear.

The mind constantly generates thoughts. The key is not to treat every thought as if it were a fact. The mind serves to organize information, solve problems, and plan. When it fulfills that function, it helps. When it starts to fabricate stories without control, it exhausts and confuses.

Learning to distinguish between "I thought this" and "this is a fact" transforms your relationship with yourself. "I can't handle this" is a thought. "I submitted the report on time yesterday" is a fact. "They always exclude me" is a thought. "They didn't call me back after the last interview" is a fact. The distinction seems obvious when written, but in your head everything blends together. Thoughts tend to shout; facts simply remain.

Rediscovering yourself requires facing discomfort without resorting to "toxic positivity" that invalidates what you feel. Using "seeing the bright side" as a cover becomes emotional camouflage that prevents genuine reckoning. The aim is balance: recognize things as they are and, from that clarity, allow a constructive interpretation if it naturally arises.

Seeing clearly means recording what you did without embellishment or justification. Yesterday you avoided that conversation, and today you fell into the same pattern again. Last week you said you would change something, and you haven't even started. These are facts—not judgments. When you see them without adding drama or guilt, what needs to change becomes evident.

This is a requirement for clear, unfiltered observation. Admitting where you stand and naming what you avoided brings both relief and precision—because that precision allows for effective movement.

But mental analysis alone is not enough; there is a deeper layer where the real blockage lies.

Disconnection rarely announces itself clearly. It appears in subtle ways: something prevents you from sitting down to write honestly; you feel irritation when someone asks, "How are you?" and you don't have an answer; or you feel the urge to distract yourself just as you approach something difficult.

Those are the signals. And they do not always appear clearly. They come as background noise, as avoidance, or as sudden emotional fatigue. Recognizing them is one of the most difficult—and necessary—parts of the work. The irritation you feel after a difficult conversation is not random; it is information. Guilt, restlessness, or insomnia are signs of a mismatch between what you present and who you are.

The deeper issue is treating emotions as problems to eliminate, when they are actually signals to be understood. Emotions must be named. When you name them—whether it is anger, fear, or even joy you do not allow yourself to feel—they stop being diffuse and become something you can act on.

What you face can be managed. What you avoid will continue to operate in the background.

You learned that certain parts of yourself "should not exist." So you suppressed them—not because they were wrong, but because they were inconvenient. The anger you hid to be "good," the boredom you disguised as laziness to be "productive," the sensitivity you concealed to appear "strong." Ignoring them did not eliminate them—it only pushed them underground, where they continue to operate.

Rediscovery asks you to go there. If you acknowledge those parts without judgment or idealization, you begin to see them clearly. Once they are no longer denied, they lose their unconscious power—and only then can you decide what to do with them consciously.

There is no manual or fixed timeline for this. It is a process of observation: writing what you see without filtering it, noticing contradictions, and naming what you have been avoiding. What matters is honesty. If you do it to feel better, it won't work; if you do it to understand yourself, everything starts to align.

This practice does not give immediate answers—it provides information. And with enough clarity, the answers emerge.

The question remains: Who are you?

Now you understand that answering it is not a one-time event—it is an ongoing practice of honest observation. Each time you return to it, the answer becomes clearer.

That is the work: to rediscover yourself again and again.

Are you willing to see yourself without the image you have constructed—even if you don't like everything you find?

THE RECORD: Writing without filters

This journal is intended as a space to see how things are, not how you would like them to be.

1. **Vitality inventory**: What did you spend energy on today that was beyond your control? What conversation or task left you feeling most disconnected? What was the reason?

2. **Fact versus story**: Write down the negative thought that repeated itself most in your mind today and ask yourself if it is a 100% verifiable fact or is it a story, you're telling yourself? What objective evidence contradicts it?

3. **Emotion as a signal**: What emotion predominated today (irritation, sadness, guilt)? Without judging it, what was that emotion telling you about a boundary you didn't set or an expectation you didn't let go of?

Pride does not defend who you are; it defends the image you have constructed so that you will be accepted.

CHAPTER 10: Stage 2 - Authenticity

You have already peeled away some layers and rediscovered parts of yourself that you had kept locked away. Now you face a pointed question: How do you live as that person in your day-to-day life?

It is one thing to recognize yourself in private and quite another to act from that place in front of the world. Your search shifts from your mind to the trenches of your everyday decisions: what you say when someone asks you something, what you keep quiet about when you should speak up, and what you accept—even if you don't want to.

Being authentic is an uncomfortable exercise in reflection that forces you to review what you do when you are alone. You have probably already felt the friction. You are in a meeting, and someone proposes something that you know will not have the desired outcome. You see it clearly: it is unfeasible, or you disagree with it. You look around and see that everyone else is nodding. Something inside you quickly calculates the price of disagreeing, the stress of having to explain it, and the risk of appearing confrontational. You nod your head, say "that makes sense" in a convincing tone, and return to your seat with the bitter certainty that you have left something unsaid.

Not only did you leave an idea hanging in the air; you left the actor who nods to fit in in charge. That discomfort stems from the dissonance between what is experienced inside and what is shown outside. It comes at a high price that is paid with weariness, tension, and the certainty of not belonging to either side.

What do you still respond to out of the old need to be accepted?

Do you continue to play a role just because the guideline feels familiar?

The figure that weighs heavily on you today was built brick by brick, by adapting to what was expected of you. You thought that certain parts of yourself were not welcome, so you kept them hidden to protect yourself. You are congratulated on the project, you smile and thank them; inside, you say to yourself, "If they knew how I did it, they wouldn't be so impressed." Or vice versa: someone criticizes your work and you feel like you're falling apart, even if the criticism is fair, because the character you built cannot tolerate imperfection.

Pride does not defend who you are; it defends the image you have constructed so that you will be accepted. That is why these strategies have become habits, and habits have become identity. The construction of this persona is the work of the ego. It acts as a survival tool that has become obsolete, even though we confuse it with an enemy.

By nature, the ego is rigid, fears disappearing, and knows only two metrics: security and approval. That is why it opposes any step or determination it cannot control. It wants you to be secure and approved, not authentic. Its main fear lies in the judgment of others, as this threatens its existence.

The rigidity and tension you carry are not flaws; they are the exhausting effort of your ego to keep an old structure standing. And when the figure fails, your ego attacks you and judges you with the same harshness with which you learned to judge others. It is not true; it is habit.

That is why the ego also blocks certain acts that it interprets as defeat: apologizing when you are wrong, admitting that you do not know, changing your mind after having defended it, asking for help when your resources are not enough. It disguises them as weakness so that you don't do them. But from a position of authority, they are exactly the opposite: they require more inner strength than clinging to your stance. Acknowledging a mistake does not diminish you; it gives you the chance to correct it. Asking for help is not giving up your power; it is using it. The ego would rather see you drown in silence than admit that you can't do it alone. Self-authority allows you to resolve.

If security is measured by how well you fit in, discomfort will be the only sign of vitality you have left. What used to be a survival mechanism is now the price of security. The "should" and "musts" have piled up like invisible bricks: you should please others, you must be efficient, you should silence what gets in the way. Without you realizing it, your own desires became suspect, and harmony became an imprudent luxury.

When you stop, the unknown that changes everything emerges: What would happen if you stepped down from the spotlight, just for a moment? If you showed what you think, what is the worst that could happen? And if you did, what's the best that could happen?

Fear is rarely just the response of others. It is something more severe: it is the fear of emptiness. We spend so much time playing the "role" that we believe that is all we are. Taking it down is like disappearing. What paralyzes us is the question, "Who will I be if I stop being this?" It's a necessary scare, because only in that void can you begin to give priority to what you want.

The energy you spend on maintaining a version that does not represent you could be used to build an environment that does reflect you. Authenticity requires consistency with what you feel, express, and do, not perfection. Being authentic is not about saying everything you think without a filter; it is about aligning with what you feel and want from a clear, grounded place. The direction lies in the internal consistency between your truth and your decisions.

People who were drawn to that compliant "you" may not recognize the new you; some will walk away, others will remain silent, and a few will come closer, recognizing what is and what is not. It will be an adjustment, even if it feels like a loss. Relationships that don't tolerate your truth weren't solid. What breaks when you are authentic is what was false. This is how you discover that not everything is worth giving yourself to and that not every union deserves to continue.

Being genuine teaches you to value things for their logic and meaning, for what they are, not for their appearance. There will be days when you fall back into your old ways, and that's okay. It's more important to realize that than to avoid making a mistake. Recognizing when you have acted against yourself makes all the difference, because before you didn't even notice it.

When you stop measuring your worth based on the praise of others, you learn to move without the disguise. And when the day ends, when everything shuts down, what remains is that truth that only you know. The one that doesn't lie. The one that knows if your actions today represented you or distanced you.

What matters is what remains when, finally, there is peace. When there are no speeches and you understand that being genuine is not about reaching a goal, it's about stopping running away.

Could you give the same answer at your dinner table as you would at a work meeting?

Are you the same person in everything you say, do, and allow—and can you recognize yourself in that consistency?

THE RECORD: The cost of the persona

Authenticity is measured by the distance between what you feel and what you show. This record seeks to measure that distance. If it helps, you can use these questions to see the cost of the role you take on in your daily life.

1. **Dissonance**: Describe a situation you have experienced today or this week in which you agreed outwardly, but inwardly you screamed "no." What was the direct price of maintaining that imposed role (tension, despondency, resentment)?

2. **The inherited script**: What "should" or "have to" guided your decisions today? Did that "should" come from you, or did you inherit it?

3. **The test**: What is the worst thing that could have happened if you had told the truth at that moment, and what is the best thing you could have gained (peace, clarity, time)? Who are you when you close the door and the audience leaves?

Clarity comes with movement; it rarely arrives beforehand.

CHAPTER 11: Stage 3 - Deployment

You have recognized who you are. You have seen the gap between what you say and what you do. You are ready to act. Don't expect grandiose acts or spectacular changes overnight. I now invite you to focus on translating what you saw into a small, concrete, and verifiable action for today, the moment when you move from observation to action.

You must discover, through action itself, whether what you recognized in theory is supported in practice. This stage is carried out as a reconnaissance exercise.

You're not signing a contract for life; you're just trying on the suit. You make a small move to see how the environment responds and how you feel. If the result doesn't fit or you don't like it, you're free to step back. It's an experiment.

The most common temptation is to procrastinate. You tell yourself, "When I have a clearer picture, I'll act." But clarity comes with movement; it rarely arrives beforehand. You can write pages about your values and repeat them aloud, but until you put them into action, they remain abstract concepts.

Without aiming for extraordinary steps, ask yourself: what is the smallest thing you are willing to do today, knowing that the pretext of perfect judgment condemns you to inaction? The first thing you discover when you begin is how unfamiliar change feels. Not only for you, but also for others. If you used to say yes to everything and now you try saying "no," someone will be confused. If you used to stay quiet and now you speak up, someone will feel uncomfortable. If you used to be available at all hours and now you choose not to be, someone may interpret it as rejection.

That reaction confirms that something has changed. The people around you became accustomed to a version of you, and when that version evolves, some celebrate it and others question it. Remember: you don't need to convince others of your progress. Nor do you need to justify every decision or ask permission to act. Your progress belongs to you and reveals itself through your actions.

Trying to demonstrate perfect honesty pushes you back into performance. Authenticity is imperfect—sometimes awkward—but always adjustable. You don't have to prove anything. It's a test, and one action is enough—one aligned with each value you defined as non-negotiable.

If your value is health, one action could be going to bed half an hour earlier. If your value is honesty, it could be correcting a statement that would otherwise become an excuse. That is enough—the essential point is that the value translates into concrete behavior.

If you say you value honesty, the minimum action is not "being more honest" in the abstract. It is something verifiable, such as: "Today, when someone asks me how I am, I will answer truthfully, even if it is uncomfortable." If you say you value your time, instead of "learning to say no," you define: "The next time I receive an invitation that doesn't interest me, I will decline it without justification."

One action, one day, one value. That is all. If it fits, you repeat it. If not, you adjust. Through repetition, you first test and then consolidate, because repetition shapes behavior. The first day is difficult, the fifth less so, and by the tenth you no longer think about it—you act. That is the difference between trying once and sustaining change.

This is the point where most people stop. Someone says something. Before, that would have made you explode, give in, or shut up. Not now. It is a brief lapse—milliseconds, imperceptible to those on the outside—that is enormous to you. In that moment, there are two options: respond from the old pattern or from what you have recognized as your own.

The same usual phrase, the same tone, the same irritation. They respond well until they stop doing so.

Recognizing this does not amplify it; it only makes it visible. And when you finally understand it, it doesn't matter if it's just once: something loosens inside. The next time it appears, you will be able to choose with different criteria.

At that point where you could react as you usually do, you instead stop, breathe, and choose.

In scenarios like this, there will be days when you act with more discernment and others when you return to old patterns. That's how progress works.

Often, a failed attempt provides more information than perfection, as it shows you exactly where its vestiges continue to work.

A stumble serves its purpose if you manage to move forward after the fall, which consolidates true restructuring.

This deployment is supported by your relationships, the environment in which you move, and how you use your time.

Now the mirror turns. What you recognize outside may also dwell within you. Reviewing what ties remain in your life also means recognizing whether you yourself are detracting from someone else's life. We are not perfect. It does not mean eliminating people as if they were obstacles; it just means rearranging the space; we have room for everyone, but not everyone occupies the same position in your current life.

Your environment can be an anchor that keeps you trapped in the old sequence or a ramp that facilitates the transition. Prepare your territory so that the new action is the easiest to carry out and the old one the most intricate. Rearranging your environment can feel like disloyalty. However, honoring what you have experienced is different from clinging to what no longer fits. There will undoubtedly be tension. Some will accuse you of being a different person. Not everyone will celebrate your consistency, because deep down, it questions their own decisions.

Finally, there is time. Every "yes" you give commits hours that you will not get back. Every "no" you say frees up intimate space for what matters to you.

If you fill your schedule with commitments that do not reflect what you want, you will hardly have room to develop what is truly yours.

The underlying question ignores how others see you and focuses on how you feel at the end of the day. If, at the end of the day, you feel the exhaustion of the work you chose, you are on the right track. If what you feel is depletion, you have probably taken on what is not meant for you.

Every step you take, every relationship you rearrange, every "no" you say, brings you back to where you've already been. It forces you to reexamine your life with new perspectives. Authenticity takes hold only when you are able to act without spectators or approval.

Ultimately, the only valid measure is your inner feeling. What small adjustment in your actions today would make that feeling lean a little more toward peace than toward depletion?

THE RECORD: The descent into the concrete

Deployment is not an idea; it is an act. Here, internal order becomes a verifiable indicator.

1. **The initial movement**: You can define a value that is "non-negotiable" for you. What step do you think you can take tomorrow to honor it?

2. **The moment of choice**: Now you might recall an automatic reaction you had today (exploding, giving in, staying silent). At what precise moment do you think you could have chosen differently? What could you do the next time it happens?

3. **Relationship inventory**: Who have you felt most disconnected from this week after talking? And how are you in the lives of others: are you the one who drains, the one who shuts down, or the one who respects space?

Understanding means integrating: the moment when something fits together without effort or conflict.

CHAPTER 12: Stage 4 - Integration

During the transition, you enter a stage in which everything you have done stops being executed in separate parts and begins to function as a cohesive whole. You see it in specific moments: you choose your words more carefully, you pause before responding, or you say a firm "no" without unnecessary justification. You stop chasing visible outcomes and allow yourself to take your place without internal conflict. Even if the environment remains difficult, that external friction no longer breaks you internally.

Where do you notice that something has been put in order, even though it is not visible from the outside?

At first glance, nothing spectacular. Inside, something has been put in order and has begun to stand firm on its own. For a long time, your attention was directed outward, hijacked by what others thought, how they reacted, and the constant doubt of whether or not you fit in. Now you return to yourself, stay, and observe. Far from being a solemn or mystical act, it is a practical way of navigating everyday life within yourself while remaining connected to the world around you.

At first, this state feels strange because you were used to constant distraction and filling pauses with interference. Stopping and listening to yourself can cause initial disorientation. However, because it is unusual, it becomes a gateway to deciding from a different way of being.

What happens inside you when you stop looking for distractions?

What do you hear when you finally find silence?

When you try to change, your current environment reacts as usual. For years, it has maintained a specific configuration, a pre-existing structure that you have accepted without questioning it too much. When you introduce something new, that structure resists. Habit tends to perpetuate itself.

What pattern have you recently returned to without realizing it, and what triggered it?

Even when you interpret it as personal failure, it is only the mold trying to maintain its familiar shape. Integration allows that structure to soften and reorganize, incorporating what you have chosen without forcing a traumatic redefinition. Sometimes the people around you resist; your rethinking shows them their own stagnation, and that can lead to a tense situation or be poorly received.

What part of your current routine would have to give way for this new thing to have a concrete place?

Changes don't happen overnight. They begin when you notice those little signs: clearer decisions, gentler reactions, firmer internal coordination. Thought, emotion, and action begin to speak the same language. Understanding becomes embodied; it is no longer just an abstract idea. Moments of clarity are no longer isolated; they become the natural course of your days. You understand the meaning of your past decisions, what you were looking for, and what hurt you, because you now recognize it in your body without the urgency to analyze it mentally.

That perspective allows everything to begin to come together. What were once loose and disconnected parts—emotion, thought, gestures—find their place and meaning. Understanding means integrating: the moment when something fits together without effort or conflict.

Integration is confirmed when a decision no longer divides you internally. Before, being consistent required managing guilt, fear, or exhausting mental debate; now, that same response, without tension, allows you to move forward without revisiting what happened, because what you think and what you feel no longer contradict each other.

When did you feel that something within you aligned without the need for explanations?

Sometimes you discover that you are acting differently without even planning to. You respond calmly where before there was impulsive reaction; you choose wisely where before there was drift. It could be that in the middle of a tense conversation, someone attacked you, and instead of defending yourself, you notice your chest expand as you inhale. Or it could be that when you checked your phone, you realized that the compulsive urge to respond had already disappeared.

This section requires honest observation guided more by direction than by perfectionism. It consists of seeing what is viable, what is failing, and what needs adjustment. The essential thing is to avoid judging the process; what has not yet found its place indicates what still needs to be integrated.

External validation loses weight and comparisons dissolve, because now you measure your progress with your own criteria. Everyday life becomes a field of verification, not public demonstration.

The form of effort changes dramatically; what once required drive and willpower is now maintained more naturally. Willpower is still present, but now it guides rather than pushes. Thinking and feeling move together.

The body joins this order. It stops reacting defensively and responds with precision. You notice it in your shoulders, which are no longer hunched in constant tension, or in your jaw, which rests without having to remind it to relax. The body ceases to be a burden and becomes an active part of the dialogue.

Even mistakes take on a different meaning; they refine you without dividing you. The difference lies in your ability to recover after falling.

On the other hand, relationships are rearranged. What was sustained solely by habit begins to adjust its dynamics.

Those who stay do so out of harmony and affinity, and those who leave do so because their time is up. There is only natural reorganization, without conquest or abrupt rupture.

Time ceases to be an enemy or a debt to be paid and becomes an environment where everything finds its place. You understand that what is essential emerges when it is ready, without the need to rush it.

Progress is measured by stability. There will be days when it seems like you are going backwards, stumbling over old habits and reactions. This time you notice it, and when you notice it, you choose differently. That ability to return supports the entire process.

You are no longer alone in front of yourself; you are with yourself. The company you once desperately sought outside becomes internal. You still need others, but you no longer abandon yourself to have them close. You learn to trust your own opinion.

What seems settled today may change tomorrow, and that is evolution. Every adjustment, every repetition, and every pause refines what you have learned. Consistency is integrated, and now transformation begins to operate on its own.

Do you allow yourself to notice these signs, or do you keep waiting for a dramatic turning point that will confirm everything?

THE RECORD: Signs of adequacy

Integration cannot be forced; it is recognized when it arrives. It is the moment when the journey ceases to be an effort and becomes your natural state of being.

1. **The unplanned expression**: What did you do this week that surprised you?

2. **The embodied criterion**: What did you "come to understand" about yourself these days? Was there a physical sensation that felt like "something had fallen into place"? What situation showed you that thought and emotion were beginning to align?

3. **Your direction**: When have you felt your body "at ease" (relaxed shoulders, deep breathing, relaxed jaw)? What were you doing (or not doing) on that occasion? How will you stay on course when external demands start to pull you in different directions again?

Waiting for total lucidity before acting is the most sophisticated state of passivity.

CHAPTER 13: Stage 5 - Action

Inevitably, you find a point within the sequence where everything you have observed demands to be materialized in a firm step. Far from requiring a public spectacle or demonstration, the situation calls for a small, strategic shift that brings you closer to your goal. Action is, in essence, movement with direction.

Turning what was previously an observation, a choice, and a practice into action requires internal guidance. It makes no sense to start walking if you don't even have an approximate direction; if the course remains an undefined illusion, the effort dissipates into sterile movement that does not generate real progress.

The distinction: acting and moving are different things. You can be very busy, full of tasks, and still go nowhere. You can fill your day answering messages, attending meetings, and checking off to-do items without moving an inch from your starting point. False moves. No useful work. No progress.

Effective action belongs to another category; it is that specific movement that you know will reconfigure things, and it is precisely because of its capacity for reconfiguration that it generates fear. We postpone it, we wrap it up in endless preparations, we talk about it or analyze it until we are immobilized. You find yourself faced with the contrast between the action you prepare for show and the move you make, even if no one finds out about it. The first seeks applause; the second seeks consequences.

What would you do if you knew no one would notice? What would you do if there were no witnesses or celebrations?

That is where your action lies. The rest is interference. Every day that passes thinking about your goal without executing anything confirms your immobility. Waiting for total lucidity before acting is the most sophisticated state of passivity.

You tell yourself, "When everything is clearer, I'll act." But clarity emerges from movement, rarely from static thinking. You take a step, and the path and context show you what to adjust. The direction is adjusted as you walk. You even avoid actions that would confirm something about yourself that you'd rather not know. You think it's fear of failure, when it's fear of what you would see if you acted appropriately. If you take that step and the result works, you can no longer tell yourself that you couldn't do it. And that excuse has served you well for years.

Sometimes "I can't" is "I don't want to" that you don't dare to say. Saying "I can't" leaves you in the position of the limited. Saying "I don't want to" puts you in the position of the chooser. And choosing makes you responsible.

Additionally, there is what you would lose if you act. Not what you would gain—you already know that, which is why it appeals to you—but what would fall apart.

Every action has a price to pay that is not visible in the fantasy. If you make that decision, what version of yourself becomes unsustainable? What relationship becomes strained? What image is shattered?

You make that calculation silently, quickly, almost without noticing. And then you tell yourself that "it's not the right time yet."

Sometimes you make specific decisions: the email you put off for fear of the response, or the file you could open to write an imperfect paragraph instead of visualizing the ideal book. Other times, you are clear about your direction, but the distance overwhelms you and the distant destination paralyzes you. Despite this, setting only the next viable step transforms tension into traction. When you only think, the unease stays with you, corrodes you, and time slips away; when you act, even if you make a mistake, something moves.

There is one factor about the first step that few mention: the obstacle is physical, not just mental. When you haven't made progress for a while, your body and mind become accustomed to inertia as a natural state. Breaking out of that state hurts; the longer you've been stuck, the greater the opposing force. If you haven't written for a month, opening the document feels like pushing against a wall.

But that blockage diminishes with each attempt. The first day is the hardest, the second not so much, and the third is already easier. This happens because repetition reminds the body that it can move. That's why the first step is the most important: it breaks the deadlock.

When you are clear about your goal and identify what brings you closer to it, you understand that not all movement counts equally. Tidying drawers instead of writing or getting caught up in emails so you don't have to make phone calls are forms of deliberate distraction. You move a lot and still don't make progress. How you feel at the end of the day is an indicator: ending up tired and unanchored indicates aimless movement; ending up exhausted but at peace indicates that what you did mattered.

The essential can be as concrete as closing the computer at the proposed time, or as human as apologizing without beating around the bush. Moving with fear is still movement. Novelty is exciting, but it doesn't last long. That's why it helps to have a daily minimum that keeps you on track; something so basic that you can do it on your worst day, when everything goes wrong and you feel like giving up.

If in the Deployment stage you tested the water temperature with your toe, checked the weather, and measured the waves, in this stage you jump in. You are no longer evaluating from the edge; you are in. There is a tipping point where all the preparation is useless if you don't commit. You can keep measuring conditions forever, but you only know the water when you get wet. That's the difference between observing and committing.

Action here requires commitment. Your "daily minimum" becomes the brick you lay each day to build the structure that will support you later.

The perfect moment—that fraction of time when you have total judgment, plenty of time, and full energy—does not exist. The perfect moment is today, with all your resources.

Your journey begins with the next conscious course of action, not in some ideal future. When you finish reading this, the option of inertia will remain, but so will the possibility of doing something. The key point is whether you choose to start, not whether you will arrive.

THE RECORD: The minimum that moves you

Action is perspective put into motion. It is not the feat that matters, but the act that breaks stagnation or passivity.

1. **Direction versus activity**: If you look at your day honestly, what task made you feel "busy" but "lost" (movement without direction)? And what act, however small, made you feel "tired" but "at peace" (movement with direction)?

2. **The price of procrastination**: What specific action have you been putting off? How much longer are you going to keep testing the water from the sidelines?

3. **Your minimum viable**: Enthusiasm fails. Discipline is not constant. What action brings you closer to your goal and can you do even on your worst day without feeling like it? What water are you going to jump into today without anyone seeing you?

What saved you in one phase may become what traps you in the next.

CHAPTER 14: Stage 6 - Reaffirmation

The precise moment when the tests begin to bear fruit is approaching. Although not everything works all the time, the truth is that something is becoming solid. You verify it physically because your state changes when you carry it out: you are lighter, clearer, more yourself.

The real question is whether you are going to make that experience part of your usual structure or leave it as an isolated anecdote.

Trying something that benefits you is different from anchoring it in your foundation. I'm talking about making it your way of being as long as it remains useful.

Let's analyze something specific, like learning to say "no." You've tried it in different scenarios. In some, declining that unnecessary meeting brought you relief. In others, a blunt "no" broke something you wanted to take care of. You can perfectly distinguish which ones felt good and which ones caused you conflict. In that distinction, you recognize yourself.

The challenge is to make what it taught you your own, repeating it until it becomes your standard.

We often confuse continuing with what works with persevering with what no longer works. Things change. What nourished you six months ago may be draining you today. Letting go of what no longer works is an essential part of keeping what really matters.

What saved you in one phase may become what traps you in the next. The boundary you set to protect yourself became the wall that isolates you. The discipline you cultivated became the rigidity that suffocates you. The independence you conquered became the inability to ask for help.

Answers often have an expiration date. What worked remains in place long after it has ceased to serve you, and you defend it because admitting that it no longer serves you feels like betraying who you were when you needed it.

What's more, you keep saying it so you don't have to admit you made a mistake in the first place. Years invested in something you knew early on wasn't part of you, but letting it go meant acknowledging that you had wasted them. But you insist and call it perseverance, when it is loyalty to a mistake you don't want to face.

There is still another trap: publicly maintaining what you have already let go of in private. You keep talking about it as if it defined you, you keep showing it because others expect to see it, even though no one lives there anymore. Consistency becomes a prison only when it sustains an empty structure solely because change would confuse those who look at you.

What are you still carrying out of loyalty to who you are no longer?

Taking a hard look at what weighs you down today prevents you from carrying unnecessary baggage.

Actions that initially required effort now come naturally. However, you carry what you thought was your own but turned out to be an external mandate. You insisted on getting up at five in the morning because it is "supposed" to be the habit of success, until one day you let it go and relief came. Prolonging certain things out of obligation prevents you from maintaining what truly reflects you. If you carry everything, you collapse the essential.

The act of consciously returning to your choice is felt in the body. This deliberate return brings order and direction, allowing you to choose again, even if you have done so a thousand times before.

At what point in your daily routines do you find yourself absent, and what does that absence tell you?

Integration is demonstrated on bad days. If you abandon the practice as soon as you encounter the first difficulty or when you don't feel like it, it's a sign that it hasn't quite taken hold yet. What you continue to choose despite inertia is what, over time, becomes solid.

When you maintain your direction with perspective, your environment adjusts. Some people come closer and others drift away. Those who were waiting for your previous version feel a little tense. Your logic speaks for itself. That distancing provides valuable information: it shows you who was with you for your complacency and who is with you for who you are.

It is important to note that the invisible work that no one applauds is in the details, in staying the course on gray days without witnesses or celebrations. What happens in the shadows surpasses what happens in public, because you do it for yourself, not to prove anything.

Inevitably, you will make mistakes in determining what to keep and what to let go. Mistakes, far from being obstacles, show you where to adjust. Accepting them as information changes your perspective. Meaning surpasses perfection.

What matters is that, while you do it, you notice it and know why you are doing it, feeling that it brings you order. And when you stop doing it, you have the discernment to let it go and try something else.

Nothing must last forever to have value.

What does an honest review of your current situation demand?

What are you holding on to that no longer serves you?

THE RECORD: Holding on to what works

Reaffirmation is the intentional choice to repeat what serves you and let go of what weighs you down. You carefully return to the essentials to strengthen your structure.

1. **What stays**: What attitude or boundary have you tried that has been useful and made you feel more like yourself? What will you do to turn that isolated experience into a deliberate practice?

2. **What goes**: What routine, bond, or belief do you continue to maintain out of habit or obligation, even though it weighs you down or drains you? What decision or boundary makes you more genuine, and what are you willing to let go of to stop carrying what does not belong to you?

Section 3 - The Friction of The Path

Relapse is not failure—it is data that shows you exactly where your conviction weakened under pressure.

CHAPTER 15: The Backlash and Relapse as Information

If you've made it this far, you already have the sequence. But having it is not the same as sustaining it. What follows is what happens when you try to apply it to a life that does not stop for you. Friction is not an exception—it is the process.

You did it. You said "no." Not a hesitant or qualified no—a clear, definitive one. For the first time, you interrupted a pattern that had operated automatically for years.

You hang up the phone expecting relief, maybe even a sense of liberation. Instead, your body reacts. A wave rises: tightness in your chest, tension in your jaw, a surge of guilt. Your immediate impulse is to undo it—to call back, apologize, and restore the previous order. This reaction is backlash.

It is not a sign that something is wrong. It is evidence that something is changing. You are not breaking—you are withdrawing from a version of yourself that no longer fits. It is the physiological response to internal honesty. It is what happens when a system is disrupted.

It is essential to distinguish backlash from a bad decision, because at first they feel identical.

Backlash is uncomfortable, but it aligns you. After the intensity passes, something settles. There is a quiet sense of coherence—a recognition that, despite the discomfort, you acted in accordance with yourself. A bad decision does the opposite. The discomfort lingers. Your body remains tense. Something in you resists not because it is unfamiliar, but because it is misaligned. The difference is revealed after the wave subsides: one leaves you closer to yourself; the other moves you further away. Backlash is tension with order—it passes. A bad decision is tension with fracture—it persists.

The first resistance you encounter is internal. Your brain is not designed for happiness—it is designed for survival. And survival favors the familiar. Even familiar discomfort is interpreted as safe. Your new "no" represents uncertainty, and uncertainty is flagged as a threat.

So the system reacts with anxiety, doubt, and urgency—all of it aimed at restoring the previous pattern. Then comes guilt.

For years, you operated under an implicit rule: being good means saying yes. Now you violate that rule. The internal conflict is immediate. The fastest way to relieve it is to reverse your action—to apologize, to comply, to return. But the work is not to eliminate guilt—it is to bear it without obeying it. You let it be there, you feel it, and you choose anyway.

The second resistance is external. Your environment had an unspoken agreement with you. You occupied a role: the one who solves, the one who accommodates, the one who does not disrupt. When you stop playing that role, the system destabilizes.

People respond. They apply pressure. Sometimes subtly, sometimes directly. They will use guilt ("After all I've done for you?"), hurtful labels ("You've become selfish"), victimhood ("You're abandoning me") or direct anger ("Who do you think you are?").

These reactions are not about you. They are about the role you abandoned.

You do not need to argue. You do not need to convince. Stability is enough.

And then, inevitably, you relapse. You say yes again. You fall back into the pattern. And your mind tries to use that moment as proof that nothing works—that is the real trap.

Relapse is not failure—it is data that shows you exactly where your conviction weakened under pressure.

The difference now is not that you never fall—it is that you see it sooner. Before, you would fall and stay there for months. Now you fall and notice it the same day. Eventually, you will notice it in real time. You will pause. You will breathe. And you will choose again. That is the process. We tend to avoid friction, but friction is what allows movement. Without it, there is no traction.

A car moves because its tires resist the road—you move because something pushes back. Guilt, pressure, resistance: none of these are obstacles. They are the conditions that make movement possible.

If you do not feel them, you are either not moving—or you are being carried.

Backlash becomes your test, and the question is not whether discomfort appears. It will. The question is whether you can move through it without abandoning yourself.

When the next wave comes—when guilt rises, when doubt tightens—what will you remember before you decide?

THE RECORD: Anatomy of relapse and backlash

1. **The internal backlash**: It may help to remember the last time you tried to set a boundary and felt guilty or anxious afterward. What was the exact "story" you told yourself to justify that guilt? Was that story a fact or a fear-driven narrative?

2. **External backlash**: What specific phrases or reactions from those around you make you doubt your transition or tempt you to return to your old role? Are those reactions for your well-being or about theirs?

3. **Relapse as information**: You can look at your latest return on an old pattern without judging yourself. What was the exact trigger? What did you feel just before you gave in? What information did that event give you that you need to reinforce? What will you do with that information? What secondary benefit did you gain from returning to your old role?

It is not effort that exhausts you—it is movement without intention.

CHAPTER 16: From Necessary Brakes to The Progress Trap

Grow, move forward, improve. You were told that stopping was a mistake and that life was about accumulating successes without pause. Today, progress has become a mandatory slogan. Behind that promise lies something hidden: the trap of moving forward without your own direction, pursuing goals that did not originate from you but were imposed by others and became unquestioned rules.

Conflict arises when improvement ceases to be a possibility and becomes a mandate. Under this relentless logic—where everything must multiply, yield, and progress—the priority shifts: it no longer matters what you build, but how much you accumulate.

Quality gives way to an obsession with quantity. What once appeared to be a path of evolution becomes a race with no finish line, as each achievement immediately generates the obligation of the next.

You complete a task and, before you can rest or celebrate, you are already planning the next one. You compare yourself relentlessly: who posts more, who earns more, who goes further. Even leisure becomes a form of performance competition.

We struggle to question this because we carry two fundamentals—but false—beliefs. The first assumes that life should follow a linear, upward trajectory, without pauses or setbacks. The second insists that more is always better. Both are wrong. Reality is cyclical, composed of expansion and necessary retreat. And "more" often subtracts—it can mean emptying yourself internally to accumulate externally.

It is like an airport conveyor belt: you move without choosing to move, because the ground carries you forward. You arrive somewhere you never decided to go, and the emptiness appears long before satisfaction. It is not effort that exhausts you—it is movement without intention.

Many people are afraid to slow down because they have internalized the belief that if they stop producing, they lose their value. They keep moving out of fear—of losing what they have built, of confronting the inner emptiness that surfaces when they stop, or of others advancing while they remain still. So they accumulate projects as if building a protective wall. From the outside, they appear unstoppable; inside, they are holding a fragile structure together.

The most ruthless message embedded in this system is permanent insufficiency—the chronic sense that nothing is ever enough.

What felt like an achievement yesterday becomes insufficient today, and you are already chasing the next objective. The present becomes a corridor—a temporary passage where everything is preparation for something else. You live in a permanent 'meanwhile' that strips the present of meaning.

If progress has become a cage, what happens when you decide to open it?

The way out requires redefining movement. Progress becomes whatever aligns with your values and makes you more coherent with yourself. From the outside, it may look the same; internally, the experience changes completely. That is why borrowed growth does not nourish you—only authentic growth brings peace, even without recognition.

Signs of misalignment become visible: you need to hide parts of yourself to keep up, or your worth depends entirely on measurable outcomes. These are signals that the system is failing.

Slowing down forces you to confront what urgency suppresses: Does what I am doing represent me? Is this goal mine—or something I adopted to belong? Does this effort honor what I value, or does it betray it? Questions like these require stillness, not acceleration. Sometimes, the most coherent response is to do less—because a well-placed pause can save years of misdirected effort.

When you stop, resistance appears: "Why stop if everything is working?" "How can you let go of something you finally achieved?" These voices are driven by fear. The real question is: Where does your loyalty lie?

There is another way to measure your life. Instead of counting achievements, you can examine how often you acted in alignment with your values—even when it was inconvenient.

Instead of counting completed tasks, you can measure consistency. Moving forward may mean exposing yourself less, protecting more, and preserving what is essential. What endures is what is cared for—not what shines the most.

If someone asks you, "What's next?", a valid answer might be: continue doing less, continue resisting, or protect what I have already chosen. The world will continue without your urgency. What will not survive, if you do not protect it, is your inner coherence.

Reality rarely demands that you do more. Sometimes it asks you to go inward enough to sustain, with dignity, what you have already chosen.

Do you dare to slow down and hold your ground, or will you continue accumulating achievements like walls that conceal your confinement?

In that space, accumulation gives way to meaning. When you release the urgency to grow outwardly, what begins to grow within?

When you stop lying to yourself, you stop lying to others.

CHAPTER 17: Radiating Coherence (The Boomerang Effect)

You have completed the six stages. What happened inside inevitably projects outward. When you stop lying to yourself, you stop lying to others. When you respect yourself, respect for others arises as a natural consequence. By living your own life, you allow others to live theirs without interference.

Progress has no end. RADIAR operates as a recurring phase that repeats itself across new situations, different conflicts, blockages you thought you had overcome, and updated versions of the same mental knots.

The difference lies in awareness: before, you lived on autopilot, unaware of when you were betraying yourself; now you feel it in your body and can turn back. You have lost the privilege of ignorance.

The mirror you no longer fog

By ceasing to demand perfection from yourself, the way you see others softens. Other people's contradictions cease to bother you because you know your own deeply. You understand that even those in front of you carry their masks, their evasions, and cycles they have not yet closed.

They are on their own evolutionary path, just as you are on yours. Their reactions no longer feel like personal attacks; you may even sense that they are going through an internal struggle. The relationship changes because you changed first.

Not everything becomes easier. There will be those who do not notice your transformation or who reject it because it unsettles them. There will be conversations that you used to avoid and now hold with clarity, and others that you discover no longer need to exist. Change resides in the environment from which you act; what the other person does with that belongs exclusively to them.

The actions no one applauds

Your new way of responding under pressure is reflected at work. Whereas before you would jump in to defend yourself, prove yourself, or justify yourself, now you pause—even if only for a moment—to determine how to proceed. You listen before you react. You say "I don't know" when you don't know. You remain silent when your input is unnecessary and acknowledge a mistake without hesitation.

That calm comes from having made peace with yourself. Every day, it reveals itself in the small details that often go unnoticed: you close a door gently instead of slamming it, you reply to a message without projecting your frustration onto the other person, you talk about someone who is absent without resorting to easy criticism.

All of this shows that what you have done has become part of you. When you live this way, you open a possibility for someone else. At some point, you will find someone who sees you calmly asserting a boundary and understands that it is possible; on the other hand, there will be those who see it as a provocation. While you cannot control how they receive it, you can control how you act.

No guarantees

Living according to your values or desires offers no guarantee that things will improve or worsen. It could be that you act in complete harmony and your close circle continues to wait for your former self. You can be honest and a bond can be broken precisely because of that honesty.

Someone may come closer or move away; this is beyond your control. What you give returns, but not necessarily in the form you expect. The decisive factor is the real test: when you give your best and the other person does not respond, when your change is not accepted, or when, instead of inspiring, it costs you a relationship you thought was secure.

This is how you discover the meaning of all this work: whether you did it to get something in return or to live in a way you can sustain when no one is watching. What you do with yourself determines the quality of your relationship with everything else. The transformation happens within you, spreads outward, and reorganizes your environment, allowing you to live a life that finally belongs to you.

Those who act from self-sufficiency do not need to impose themselves.

CHAPTER 18: Radical Respect (Coexistence Without Invasion)

When taking care of yourself ceases to be a theoretical slogan and becomes an effective practice, the other person ceases to be a threat and becomes simply another person. From that position, coexistence depends largely on non-invasive behavior rather than on a coincidence of views. That is respect.

Respect serves as the basis for shared freedom; it involves recognizing that no one possesses absolute truth and that coexistence is possible without the need to subjugate others. Empathy makes the effort to understand why you think the way you do; respect goes a step further by recognizing your right to think differently, even in disagreement.

A lack of genuine consideration has been normalized under the guise of "tolerance."

Recognition operates from a different angle, as it accepts from the outset that you have as much right as I do to exist and to choose from a different standpoint.

For those who still feel disordered inside, imposing themselves becomes necessary to feel worthy. It is their existential emptiness they are trying to fill. Intruding through noise, opinions, or uninvited visibility becomes the most common way of confirming one's existence when something inside still feels lacking.

On social media, conversation becomes a boxing ring where people read to find each other's weak points rather than to understand each other. Indignation holds you in place; calmness lets go; and polarization, while profitable, impoverishes dialogue.

The invasion transcends the digital and extends into the physical. You're in a hospital waiting room, at a doctor's office, or at work, and someone starts playing videos on their phone at full volume. No one asked for it, yet everyone is forced to listen. The same happens in public leisure spaces, where you may have gone in search of peace and quiet, and suddenly a loudspeaker imposes its own soundtrack, erasing the shared atmosphere. If anyone dares to point this out, the response is often to increase the volume even more—doubling down.

Loud volume, messages that demand an immediate response, winning every argument—these are all symptoms of the same root. Those who act from self-sufficiency do not need to impose themselves. They allow themselves to breathe because they have already given themselves what they once sought from others.

In such situations, it is easy to see yourself as a victim. However, you must ask yourself when you have been the one who has polluted the shared space in some way, with noise or other forms of intrusion, under the justification of "you have the right to do what you want" or indifference toward the environment.

Putting your own house in order begins with every shared space, however small, rather than with grand speeches about the planet.

We are living through a historic moment in terms of technology. We can talk to someone on the other side of the world, access almost any data in seconds, and automate complex tasks. While tools evolve, human interaction deteriorates.

Little by little, basic manners, consideration for others, and the ability to be present are being lost. The contrast is clear: the more sophisticated the tools, the easier it becomes to forget the basics of how to treat one another. Technology amplifies what we do with it; the risk lies in forgetting the fundamentals while using it.

It is worth stopping to observe how you greet others, whether you look at the person in front of you, whether you are aware of what is happening in a conversation, whether you stop losing yourself in the screen, whether you take care of the shared environment, or whether you remember that on the other side of the device there is someone like you.

By distancing ourselves from what is essential and from each other, we normalize a way of life where everything is expected immediately, turning any delay into a fault and impatience into a habit. Haste has become the norm. We live under the logic of immediate response: you send a message and, if you don't receive a reply within minutes, suspicion arises. This constant immediacy turns any pause into an offense and any silence into a conflict. We confuse availability with interest and respect with immediacy, ignoring that the other person may be busy—or may simply choose not to respond.

Have we really lost the ability to be empathetic, or have we simply stopped practicing it?

Here the circle closes. Inner work eventually radiates outward. When you stop acting from a position of lack, your way of relating to others naturally shifts. It is not discipline or etiquette—it is the natural consequence of being able to sustain yourself.

The real revolution is silent: when enough individuals bring order to their inner lives, coexistence is redefined without imposed rules. Collective change begins with each individual.

Respect is demonstrated through daily actions, not ideas. Observe the environment you share: do you care for it or invade it? Practicing respect requires patience and self-trust. Coexisting without invading is enough; there is no need to defeat anyone or engage in conflict. Ultimately, it requires recognizing one another as equals—as people—beyond agreement.

What specific act of respect are you willing to practice today, knowing that the way you treat others defines the extent of your freedom?

A value counts when you're willing to defend it, even when it costs you... Everything else is rhetoric.

CHAPTER 19: Expectations, Silent and Non-Negotiable Contracts

What you expect from others is based on very specific episodes. You know what you would do if someone confided in you: you would avoid endangering anyone's life, you would use the trust placed in you to care for others rather than to gain advantage, you would keep your word, and you would protect what had been entrusted to you.

When you expect loyalty, it is because you would give it; when you expect discretion, you assume that the other person would remain silent just as you would, even when it would be in their interest to speak up. You expect someone to take care of what you have entrusted to them—a conversation, a project, a dream—because you would take care of it through your actions.

Those expectations speak to your internal structure. They show what you consider basic, what red lines are uncrossable, and what actions you consider unthinkable. What is common sense to you seems so obvious that you don't even mention it; explaining why certain things are not done seems exaggerated, almost offensive.

That's where the problem begins. We assume that others are built with the same internal program and see the same things we do. And, because we assume this, we say nothing. We stop naming what is sacred because we consider it unnecessary. This mixture of assumption and silence creates the silent contract: an agreement you sign alone, convinced that the other person thinks and feels as you do, even though no one has discussed it.

When the other person acts according to their own codes and crosses a line that they don't have, you experience that action as a betrayal. They feel that they haven't done anything serious, but you feel that they have broken something irreparable. At that moment, trust is broken and, above all, the illusion of compatibility. You discover that the other person operates differently and that what is untouchable for you was optional for them.

That discovery affects you in a very particular way. Often there is no intention to hurt; it is just someone acting normally, without measuring the weight that action had for you. Anger or helplessness mix with confusion, and it is difficult to name what happened, because it is delicate to accuse someone of bad faith when they did not even know they were crossing a boundary.

Has anyone ever crossed a line that you didn't think needed to be explained out loud?

The first reaction is usually shock: surprise, anger, a feeling of helplessness. After the impact, something useful is revealed: information. That person has just shown you how they resolve things through their actions, with what they did when they had the opportunity to choose a course. They have shown you what they are unaware of, what they do not see, and what is weightless in their internal balance.

Rather than reducing everything to whether they are a "good" or "bad" person, it is more useful to examine it from a behavioral perspective: does their way of acting align with yours?

People are divided between those who can maintain a relationship where your boundaries fit and those who cannot. What you discover is distance—the contrast between their way of being in the world and yours. That distance was already there; it has just become visible.

Recognizing the signs

The silent contract rarely originates overnight. There were previous signs: passing comments, how they address and talk about other people, how they handle what has been entrusted to them, or how they react when something suits them, even if it is wrong. Small details that we often choose to minimize to move forward without questioning the relationship.

When they finally do something you can no longer ignore and it still affects you, the surprise is relative. Somewhere inside, you already knew it; you likely saw it in the details you chose to ignore to avoid deciding between speaking up, setting a boundary, or walking away. Addressing those signs directly is an act of honesty with yourself, not paranoia.

What patterns do you continue to justify that clash head-on with what you say you value? What details are you overlooking so you don't have to decide?

Adjusting expectations

Controlling how the other person acts is beyond your control. What is within your control is the answer to a simple but critical question: what are you going to do with what you know now?

You can insist on expecting something from that person that they cannot or will not give you. That option maintains the silent contract, connecting you to the idealized version you created, which is different from the person in front of you. Or you can adjust your expectations to the reality of their actions. That does not lower your standards. You stop expecting pears from a tree that does not bear them.

Sometimes, the adjustment is practical: you stop confiding certain things to them, you limit their access to your life, and you better measure how far you go. Other times, the adjustment is radical: you choose to distance yourself, without resentment, because staying would mean betraying yourself or accepting a relationship that requires you to sacrifice too much of what is essential.

Our blind spots

So far, it's easy to think about others. However, there is another side that we often overlook: we can be someone else's "other."

We have also crossed boundaries without realizing it, used information we thought was harmless, or minimized something vital to someone else; we have even disappointed others unintentionally.

When you find yourself in that situation, you may feel tempted to justify yourself: "I didn't know," "I didn't imagine that...," "If I had known, I wouldn't have done it." These are the same phrases that sound insufficient to you when they are said to you.

Repairing your own blind spots makes you more consistent and aware. It reminds you that you are not the moral center of the universe and that, like everyone else, you are learning to measure the impact of your actions on others.

The next time someone crosses one of your boundaries, you will be able to see, along with the pain, your shared humanity: we are all capable of hurting others without realizing it. It becomes an opportunity to place yourself in the other person's position.

Define your non-negotiables

During all this, you have identified what is non-negotiable for you: the values and boundaries you are not willing to sacrifice to maintain a relationship, a project, or a sense of belonging. They serve as a reminder to you and are not merely a list of requirements for others; they are your limits.

Non-negotiables mark the point beyond which, if you continue to give in, you stop recognizing and respecting yourself. Every time you bend one of your principles "just this once," the relationship seems to win, but you lose something of yourself.

It is not immediate; it accumulates gradually. You give in to a comment, a lack of respect, a betrayal, a serious omission. You call it tolerance, patience, or judgment.

One day, the cost becomes clear; you look at yourself and do not understand how you could have gotten used to less than what you consider worthy. That's when you start to define what your true non-negotiables are.

A value counts when you're willing to defend it, even when it costs you: losing a relationship, giving up an opportunity, being left out. Everything else is rhetoric.

You could ask yourself honestly: do you apply them in both directions? Demanding respect, care, and loyalty requires you to offer them with the same consistency.

Relationships without silent contracts

Breaking free of these kinds of contracts is different from becoming distrustful or closing yourself off. The answer is simpler than we think: speak clearly and listen genuinely. Speaking clearly means daring to express what matters to you directly and honestly, without exaggerating, without defensiveness, and without expecting the other person to guess.

It means stepping away from assumptions. For example: "For me, this is a limit," "I can't do this," "If this happens, I'm going to walk away." It may be uncomfortable, but it saves years of misunderstandings.

Listening genuinely allows the other person to express their own boundaries as well, even if they don't match yours. Sometimes you'll find that they're compatible and you can build something on that basis. Other times, you'll see that the distance is too great. In both cases, the decision is an act of respect because no one is signing an invisible contract; both of you know what you're choosing.

Self-authority comes into play both in big decisions and in managing assumptions in relationships. You decide whether to continue signing agreements that the other person did not sign or whether to dare to build relationships where what is important is said, heard, and supported.

In the end, what you do with your expectations matters more than what you expect from others: do you turn it into a silent contract that leaves you at the mercy of disappointment, or into an agreement where you can be yourself without betraying yourself or others?

Understanding the nature of these contracts is the final bridge between your inner truth and the outside world.

Personal authority is only complete when you stop asking for permission to be who you are, even in your closest relationships, and dare to uphold your non-negotiables in front of others. With the map of your relationships cleared of assumptions, you are faced with the definitive fact: full responsibility for your direction, without the refuge of ignorance.

The harsh truth is that there is no happy ending; all there is is continuous and deliberate choice.

The Final Act of Choice

You have just closed a roadmap, not a storybook. Here you will not find definitive calm or a permanent solution to your problems or conflicts. This book is not a vaccine against inertia; its effect wears off if you don't apply it. What you have in your hands is a tool, a guiding instrument to be used precisely when the character tries to take over the role again.

Probably, the illusion of a happy ending is what brought you here. However, the harsh truth is that there is no happy ending; all there is is continuous and deliberate choice.

Tomorrow, when you wake up, your environment will remain the same. External demands will not have decreased, and the temptation to revert to your old role will be very strong, because it is more comfortable and familiar.

The difference is that now ignorance is no longer a valid excuse. Before, you obeyed because you couldn't see the strings that were pulling you; now you can see and feel them.

The key is this: you return to your present with your trajectory in hand. You will often give preference to the easy answer again, you will feel confusion, and you will recognize the price to pay. The work will consist of recognizing the trap more quickly and stepping out of it as soon as possible, rather than avoiding the mistake altogether.

Staying the course requires a strength that does not announce itself. It will be the tenacity of ordinary days, far from the euphoria of the beginning, when there will be moments when obedience will seem like a tempting relief from the exhausting responsibility of deciding.

But make no mistake: the relief of obeying lasts only a minute; the price of betraying yourself stays with you. Your only valid metric for measuring success is your self-command, not wealth or external recognition. It is that state of fulfillment, difficult to explain in words, but immediately recognizable when you experience it.

Every day is a new opportunity to either buy or sell your autonomy. Your ego will tell you to sell it in exchange for security. Society will pressure you to do so in exchange for acceptance. This is a reminder so that you can respond firmly that "the price is too high."

The loss of authority feels like a slow erosion of self-confidence.

The revolution of respect we discussed ceases to be a theory and becomes the result of enough individuals coexisting who choose their truth without imposing it. Respect becomes the inevitable outcome of honesty, not a moral luxury.

The plan is in your hands. The life you have, with its imperfections, frictions, and challenges, is this one. It is irrelevant whether the path will be easy. The question is whether your life will be better if you don't walk it.

Choose.

Acknowledgments

To Sebastián, for always supporting me, even when this book was just an idea.

To Teresa Baró, for the honor of her time and generosity, and for the privilege of having her write the foreword.

To my family and friends.

To all the people I have met over the years: those who were a guiding light and those who were a warning, those who opened doors and those who closed them. This book was written with all of them in mind.

Glossary Of Key Concepts

ACTION: Directional movement (Stage 5). It is the specific and strategic step that breaks the deadlock and brings you closer to your desired goal. It transforms uncertainty into traction through commitment, even when fear is still present.

AUTHENTICITY: Consistency between what you feel and what you do (Stage 2). It is the ability to assume the cost of your truth and choose from a clear, grounded place. It is measured by the decrease in internal tension.

BACKLASH: The visceral reaction (anxiety, guilt, panic) that appears after making a liberating decision. It is the "withdrawal syndrome" from the old identity and physical proof that the system has been successfully altered.

COST OF NOT CHOOSING, THE: It is the invisible price of passivity. It is the internal fracture that occurs every time a decision is delegated to others or to time. It entails the renunciation of personal responsibility and, with it, personal agency. It is paid for with the loss of one's own identity to sustain someone else's life.

DEPLOYMENT: The materialization of theory (Stage 3). It consists of translating the plan into a minimal and verifiable act to test the soundness of one's own truth when confronted with reality.

DISCERNMENT: The ability to identify the nature of stillness. It distinguishes prudence (mature waiting) from fear (paralysis) through honest analysis of decision history.

FOREIGN SCRIPTS: Schemes for success inherited from family or society. Compliance guarantees external approval, but at the cost of incongruity from living someone else's life.

FRICTION: The resistance necessary to move forward. It is contact with certain circumstances (internal guilt, environment, etc.) that provides the traction to move, just as wheels require friction against the asphalt to turn.

GURU WHO NEEDS YOU LOST, THE: A figure or system whose business is based on the inadequacy of the individual. They market magic formulas to maintain a period of dependence and nullify the follower's own judgment.

INTEGRATION: The state of fluidity in change (Stage 4). It occurs when the new way of acting becomes natural and the right decision arises without mental debate. External friction still exists, but it no longer fractures you inside.

LIMITED BALANCE: The concrete nature of time and vital energy. These are finite resources that are spent without return. It requires conscious living to invest capital in what is essential.

MINIMUM THAT MOVES YOU (MINIMUM VIABLE): The action that can be executed even on the worst day. It is the basic strategy for overcoming inconsistency and building discipline regardless of motivation.

NON-NEGOTIABLES: The limits that define personal dignity. These are the values that are defended by accepting the sacrifice of losing a relationship, job, or money to avoid self-betrayal.

PERSONAL AUTHORITY: The supreme authority over one's own life. It is the ability to decide, act, and accept the consequences based on exclusive internal validation. It is not granted from outside, it is reclaimed.

PROGRESS TRAP: The belief that one must always be "improving" or producing more. It forces one to live in the future and empties the interior to fill external expectations of infinite growth.

RADIAR: In the context of the process, this means ceasing to be a passive receiver of external signals and becoming an active transmitter of one's own frequency. It is the ability to project internal order with such clarity that one's identity organizes the environment without the need to impose, convince, or explain.

RADIATING COHERENCE: The principle of internal projection. By putting your inner world in order, your decisions and boundaries naturally radiate outward. This new configuration inevitably modifies your environment, although not always in the way you had imagined.

RADICAL RESPECT: The basis of adult coexistence. It accepts the right of others to be different and allows coexistence based on the premise of non-invasion.

REAFFIRMATION: The conscious decision to standardize well-being (Stage 6). It turns what is good for you into a habitual structure and allows you to let go of what has already run its course.

RECORD, THE: The landing tool. An unfiltered writing space designed to reformulate abstract reflection into concrete data about the state of things. It is the antidote to passive reading.

REDISCOVERY: The act of removing layers of adaptation (Stage 1). Figuratively speaking, it is looking in the mirror to see who you truly are and what you want when no one is watching, and you are no longer trying to please anyone.

RELAPSE AS INFORMATION: The stumble seen as useful data. It points to the exact point where conviction was weaker than habit, allowing you to adapt your strategy for the next attempt.

SAFE TERRITORY: Attachment to the familiar simply because it is predictable. It is the inertia that confuses familiarity and the absence of risk with happiness or peace.

SELF-COMMAND (EFFECTIVE METRIC): The only valid measure of success. It is the ability to uphold your criteria and boundaries in the face of external pressure, prioritizing internal cohesion over wealth or recognition.

SILENT CONTRACTS: Imaginary agreements signed alone. They arise when you assume that the other person shares the same codes and values without having discussed them. They are one of the most frequent sources of disappointment and feelings of betrayal in relationships.

UNDERLYING FORCES: Internal defense mechanisms (fear, loyalty, habit) that are activated when faced with the possibility of change. These are old responses that protected us in the past but now hinder our autonomy.

About The Author

Andrea Alvarado trained as a lawyer and is an entrepreneur. Her time in law gave her intellectual discipline, analytical rigor, and consideration for what others overlook.

RADIAR was born from that perspective: observing, distinguishing, and understanding dynamics of change—both personal and external—with the certainty that the only valid authority is internal.

It does not seek to teach. It is written for those who prefer to think and ask questions rather than follow formulas or accept promises of quick fixes.

If this work has left you thinking and you want to follow the thread, you can scan this code.

It will take you to a site where you will find related content and updates that will be posted from here on out.

www.ingramcontent.com/pod-product-compliance
Lightning Source LLC
LaVergne TN
LVHW090515110826
845146LV00003B/867

* 9 7 9 8 9 9 3 7 8 4 2 4 3 *